LOVE&CARE

LOVE&CARE

SHAUN DEENEY

ENDEAVOUR

First published in Great Britain in 2021 by Endeavour,
an imprint of
Octopus Publishing Group Ltd
Carmelite House
50 Victoria Embankment
London EC4Y 0DZ
www.octopusbooks.co.uk

An Hachette UK Company
www.hachette.co.uk

ISBN 978-1-91306-846-2

A CIP catalogue record for this book is available from the
British Library.

Printed and bound in Great Britain

10 9 8 7 6 5 4 3 2 1

This FSC® label means that materials used for the product
have been responsibly sourced

Some names and identifying details of characters
in this book have been changed.

For Megan and Leah,
Karen and Pam

'For it's so clear that in order to begin to live in the present we must first redeem the past, and that can only be done by suffering, by strenuous, uninterrupted labour.'

ANTON CHEKHOV, *THE CHERRY ORCHARD*, ACT II
TRANSLATED BY JULIUS WEST

'If you tell people the truth, make them laugh or they'll kill you.'

GEORGE BERNARD SHAW

BEFORE

I hold my mother under each arm as she takes tiny shuffling steps towards the car, and open the passenger door to ease her slowly back onto the seat. I lift her skinny legs one by one into the footwell and make sure her slippered feet are flat on the floor.

'Where are we going?' she asks, as I lean over to buckle her seat belt.

'For a rest,' I say, 'to a nice place. With your own room.'

'Why?'

I can't tell her why. So I lie and say this will only be for a week or two, just to give her a break. 'Like a hotel.'

The care home is a 1930s red-brick building with turrets, no doubt built as a grand home for a wealthy family. A carer meets us in reception and leads us through to the day room.

The residents sit in high-backed chairs, homogenized and diminished by age. Many are huddled beneath blankets with their heads bowed in sleep, but as we pass a woman in a tweed skirt with neatly bobbed hair and the earnest face of a teacher, she reaches out, her voice pleading. 'Nurse! Nurse! What should I be doing?' A man on a gurney, his arms writhing, is shouting, his voice shrill and echoing through a space that is otherwise oddly silent.

The carer leads us to a vacant chair tucked away beyond a baby grand piano under a green cover. Together, the two of us try to settle Mum in, though she stiffens and resists as we ease her backwards to sit. The carer brings a dining-room chair for me and offers us tea. When she goes, I try to think of something reassuring to say to Mum, but the thought of my own complicity in bringing her to this place chokes my words. How have I allowed things to come to this? Why didn't I do more?

Three weeks earlier, I had been called to an emergency meeting with adult protection services, social workers and the police. They examined the written reports from social services detailing my father's treatment of my mother – he was not physically violent, but there was evidence of neglect and rough handling – and I told them about my own experience of his cruelties and controlling behaviour over many years, beginning long before her diagnosis of Parkinson's dementia. The ten or more officials around the horseshoe-shaped conference table, some in uniform, were sober and serious as they listened to me and read from the papers in front of them. There was more discussion that did not include me, and then the head of adult protection said the only possible course of action was to remove my mother from potential harm. He made it clear that because she lacked the 'mental capacity' to bring a formal complaint against her husband of fifty years, neither social services nor the police could act unless I could persuade my father to give his permission for her to go into a care home.

And so, with no other choice, we circled him. By citing his heroic efforts to take care of his wife, the sacrifices he was making for her and the impact on his own health, I flattered and then cajoled him into agreeing to a short respite stay for my mother. The official intention was to address the situation and to ensure adequate safeguards were put in place to protect her in her own home. But I knew, and I think the authorities did too, that my father would never change, and that Mum's move to the care home would very likely be permanent.

The carer smiles reassuringly as she returns, wheeling the tea and a piece of cake towards us on a laminated hospital table. She tells me her name is Cai. She offers to sit with my mother while I take her bags up to her room.

'Go, go,' she says. 'Mum is okay with me.'

The room is cold. It has a hospital bed, a wardrobe, a dresser, and a small window overlooking the garden. The en-suite bathroom has handrails and a shower chair and is even colder than the bedroom, and though there's nothing to object to – the place is clean and uncluttered, with plain magnolia walls – there is little to love. I unpack my mother's dresses and cardigans, checking I've labelled everything with her initials in black permanent marker before hanging them in the pine wardrobe. I put a few photos of the family on the dresser and two pairs of shoes under the bed.

When I go downstairs again, Mum is alone in her chair, her tea half drunk and an empty plate with cake crumbs in front of her. I sit beside her and tell her I've put her things away. I say the room is lovely, but as I lift the wing-handled plastic cup to her mouth, I see her bottom lip is quivering and her eyes are darting this way and that, hunting for threats. I notice she is trying to speak, but her voice is weak and soft and I can't make out the words.

'What is it, Mum?'

'I want to go … to go …' she says, stumbling over her words, '… home now.'

The profound simplicity of her plea stuns me. I can think of nothing to say. At least nothing that is true. So I tell her we *will* go home, in a few days, and that meanwhile she should think of this as a holiday. I spend another hour talking about anything I can think of to distract her – my two daughters, work, the weather outside – but nothing consoles her, not even when I say I'll be back in the morning to spend the day with her. I feel certain she sees through it all. She knows this is not a holiday. Even with the fog of dementia, she understands it is all wrong. She knows she has been taken from her home and her husband and all that is familiar. What she doesn't understand is why.

The time comes for me to leave. I ask another of the carers to sit with her. I kiss my mother on the forehead, and her face creases with emotion. She is stumbling over her words, but I hear 'Don't … don't … don't …' repeated over and over as I walk away.

By the time I reach the lobby, I see the carer on her haunches in front of Mum, patting her hand, and my mother with tears rolling down her cheeks. I feel my heart breaking.

WINTER

I

It was late November, eighteen months after I had taken
my mother to the care home, when I got a call to tell me
my father was dying.

I was sitting in the shade of the medieval arches of
a bar in the middle of the Sommières Saturday market.
The midday sun of the south of France was as hot as an
English summer scorcher. The sky was entirely cloudless
and the brightest of blues. The carafe of cheap rosé I'd
ordered, as I always did on my weekends off, was down
to the last glass.

'He's in hospital again … and he's not eating at all …'

It was Brenda, who ran the care agency that had been
looking after my father since my mother had gone into
the home. She called me from time to time so I could
keep tabs on him without our having to speak in person.
I was used to tales of his bad behaviour, poor eating
habits and refusal to leave his bed.

I had been living in France for the best part of a year, sharing a broken-down farmhouse with my oldest friend Phil, an architect, working on a house he had designed and using my spare hours to write a book. I had been back to England four times to visit my mother in the care home, but I had cut off all contact with my father. For years I'd tried to buffer his worst excesses. Now, with my mother safely out of his reach, I was free of all that. Friends and family had long ago given up on him, and he was alone in his house, save for three visits a day from carers, who would try to get him to eat and see to his personal hygiene. Angry with me for having deserted him, as he saw it, he told anyone who would listen that I was a menace and very likely bipolar. I don't think it ever occurred to him that it might be his own mental health that was the problem.

'Perhaps you should think about coming back,' Brenda said. 'I have to tell you, I don't think your dad will be going home this time.'

We said our goodbyes and I poured the remains of the rosé into the glass. The tables around me were heaving with chattering customers, their tables littered with the shells of oysters bought from the market. Waiters squeezed through the crowds with trays of carafes and glasses. After a long week's work on the building site with only Phil for company, I came to this bar for the people and the bustle of life, but all at once I felt isolated and alone.

I had seen the deterioration in my mother on my visits to her in the care home. The progressive effects of Parkinson's dementia had made her frail, and she was now unable to stand or walk or feed herself. But it was also her spirit that was sick. She had been taken from all she knew, her husband and her home – I carried my own burden of guilt for that – and I knew she felt that loss every day, because when I sat with her in the day room, she would beg me not to forget her and not to leave her there. I had accepted from the very first day that Mum would likely end her days in the care home. Still, I had made promises that I would one day bring her home. I hated myself for doing so, and I never thought for a moment that those promises might come true.

All I could understand about my father's impending fate was that everything would change because of it. I didn't want to go, but I knew I would book a ticket as soon as I got back to Phil's farmhouse. Though what this trip would hold – for me, for my father, and though I hardly dared voice the thought, for my mother – was too much to take in.

And yet this was supposed to be my time. I had done what I could for others. I had survived divorce and given up my career as a television producer to work in a local off-licence so I could be there for my two young daughters, who were six and twelve at the time. I had been through the break-up of a long and loving relationship with my post-divorce partner, Marie, and still I'd carried on writing, surviving on my dwindling cash in the bank and a variety of part-time jobs – as a psychology teacher and a paella chef, as ground crew helping to launch and recover hot air balloons on pleasure trips – until finally I ran out of money and into a brick wall very like full-blown depression.

I had come to France to make a fresh start. By working with Phil and living in his farmhouse, I had just enough money to survive. My girls, now grown up, had been to visit several times, and I could finally finish my book. I was free and single, and although I was in my mid fifties, I was still hoping I might find love once more. Now, history was repeating itself, and once again I was being dragged back by all I had left behind.

I take a cab from the airport to my parents' deserted bungalow in the Surrey suburbs, arriving just as dusk is turning to night. A frost is already forming on the pavements and the lawn. I have a key because I have been here so many times before, but never to an empty house.

Inside, it is dark and cold. I see the door to my father's bedroom is open but the heavy lined curtains are closed. The blankets on his double bed are thrown back and dishevelled, as if he's only just been wheeled to the waiting ambulance. There are used tissues on the floor. His portable Roberts radio is on the cabinet by the bed, aerial extended. There is the scent of old man.

This is his home, with his things. The reproduction paintings in the front room reflect his taste for bucolic Constable prints, scenes of Cavaliers carousing, and picturesque Dutch windmills in soft evening light. The dark-wood sofa and armchairs padded with squeaky faux leather are his idea of luxury. The glass cabinets in the dining room are brimming with Waterford crystal and dotted with model aeroplanes on cheap plastic stands, along with his golf trophies.

My mother lived here too, and not long ago, but there is no sign of her, nothing she once loved or cherished, or that truly speaks of her. Her role as wife and mother was always to support my father. She was confined to the background, an attendant to my father's needs and desires, long before the ravages of Parkinson's dementia undermined her ability to express herself in words or actions. She was quiet and competent, sweeping behind us all, ready with plasters to salve a graze, a consoling hug for school reports, a favourite dish – lemon meringue pie with home-made pastry so buttery it makes my mouth water even now. But she never talked of her own needs, and when I was a boy, I took her for granted entirely. If I had rowed with Dad, she would come to me in my room when things had died down, bringing a treat to keep secret, finger to her lips to shush me, and always with that smile of hers, a smile of forbearance and infinite understanding, the smile I have so seldom seen in recent years.

As a grown man, still ignorant of her real needs, I would ask her what she might like as a present for Christmas or birthdays. She would say, 'There's nothing I need. Don't spend your money on me.' When I probed, she would struggle to come up with something for the kitchen or the garden, saying, 'Your father thinks we should have …' I would hug her and tell her she was a saint and buy her ridiculous bath oils, or a silk scarf, or a Georgette Heyer novel in hardback.

Mum has been gone from here for almost two years, and yet her single bedroom is still littered with the paraphernalia of incontinence pads and wipes. Her clothes, the photographs that were once here on the chest of drawers, and the hairbrush she loved, all these things I took to the care home, but otherwise the room is as I remember it only two years ago. Two or three times I came to stay for weekends to help care for her, but my father did not like my being here and told me not to come again. I recall holding her under both arms as we returned from the bathroom and easing her back to sit on the bed. Changing her into her nightdress and then helping her to lie down, lifting her legs as my father stood by exhorting me to 'Use the handrail, that's what it's there for.' He had had a workman screw it to the wall, but my mother could never reach it by herself. That always made him angry with her.

I clear away the mountains of medications, find some sheets and pillows and a duvet and make myself a bed for the night. I turn the central heating up high, acutely conscious of being the only living being in the house. In the kitchen, the fridge is all but empty, and I didn't stop for food on the way from the airport. Then I remember the wine rack in the garage. I squeeze past the red Honda Jazz with black leather seats my father bought new and never drove. He used the money my mother had inherited from her own mother to buy the car, just as the doctor insisted that he should give up his licence. I make a mental note to put the battery on charge. There's a thin film of dust on the paintwork, thicker dust on the wine bottles and on the golf clubs in their bag, leaning against the rack. I take two bottles back to the kitchen in the hope of finding one that isn't oxidized, but I have to empty both down the sink. There's some whisky, so I pour myself a shot and add a little water.

This bungalow was never the family home. When my parents moved here in their retirement, my sister and I were long gone, with lives of our own. There are only one or two memories that attach to the things in it: a gadget for opening the lids of jam jars I noticed just now in the kitchen drawer, for example. Its gears and extending lever fascinated me as a boy. There is a wooden pestle and mortar, ornamental and never used. The old Sinatra records have gone, along with the record player. No more *Pennies from Heaven* with Frank and Count Basie on the cover. The cheap plaster bust of JFK, its chipped shoulder glued but showing the crack, and the hardback copy of James Joyce's *Ulysses*, one of the two books my father owned – the other was Leon Uris's *Trinity* – those things have gone too, who knows where.

I feel a quite irrational irritation that there is so little here for me to remember. Those missing objects would have helped me feel more connected to this house, to my parents, and to the unfolding drama that has dragged me back into their lives. My relationship with our shared past, and indeed much of my own past, is one of a man waking from a dream, events fading as fast as my eyes blink open, leaving only mirages, a vague atmosphere, an emotion untethered from any coherent narrative. The mind is a wonderful instrument, but my memory makes only a childish collage of all that actually happened, and does so with scant regard for the truth. So little survives intact through all their many house moves and their shift to another continent.

My parents emigrated to America on my eighteenth birthday, the day after Elvis Presley died. I refused to go with them. I said America was a heathen land – to my shame, those were my exact words – with no social security system worth talking about and no health system fit for purpose. My father wanted me to study business. I told him I would study English literature, in England, because I wanted to be a writer. He didn't laugh in my face, but he did make it clear he would not give me a penny in support. I said that was fine by me. For a long time, we only saw each other for brief holidays. Things were better like that.

My sister was only sixteen when they left and was too young to see the move as anything but an adventure. We were always close, but we had separate lives, though we would keep that closeness through the years to come, despite living on different continents. She had just completed her O levels, and she went straight into an American high school the likes of which she had only seen in movies such as *Grease*. I went to university in Kent, and immersed myself in modern poetry and philosophy, beer and marijuana. Meanwhile, my sister, made exotic with her English accent, was dating a star of the school football team. She didn't fight with my father as I had as a teenager, perhaps because, as his daughter, she escaped his desire to mould her in his image. It was enough for him that she was happy to be with them in America, and settling well; so well that she would go on to make a life for herself there, and later in Canada.

They set up home in the suburbs of Washington, DC, where my father became general manager at National Airport, responsible for the company's operations. My mother found part-time work at the local county offices. She had always worked, as well as being a wife and mother, for as long as I could remember. But when, more than a decade after going to America, my father's career ended in the ignominy of demotion and redundancy, he and my mother sold, or gave away, everything they owned, including our old Labrador, and limped back to the UK. It was 1989. They were in their late fifties, and if my mother was happy to be closer to her mother and to me, my father was a defeated man. His American dream had been shattered. He suffered a nervous collapse and a severe depression that left him bedridden for a year or more. That was the first time he took to his bed. Unable to come to terms with what had happened, or to see that some things in life were mere accident, he turned his bitterness and disappointment on his family and friends, but especially on his wife.

When my mother was diagnosed with Parkinson's dementia, his depression turned to anger. What went on behind closed doors showed itself from time to time and was repellent, though there was little I could do about the petty cruelties, mad rages and anxiety attacks, other than learn to live with them and protect my mother as best I could. The golf club might have been a refuge for him, but in latter times his treatment of my mother came to the attention of other members and made it hard for him to find playing partners. Family gatherings were excruciating. I remember an occasion when I met my parents at a pub with my daughters, who were young at the time. My father insulted my mother repeatedly, telling her she was useless to him and a burden. I said I would not have my children listen to such talk and we started to leave, but my mother begged me to stay, fearing the consequences of being alone with him when he was so angry.

As her dementia progressed, he justified locking her in her room as it being for her own safety. He banned friends and family from seeing her. He point-blank refused to allow anyone to look after her in order to give them both a break, even for a weekend. He needed the burden of her care to explain his own misery. I forced the issue when I could, spending hours on the phone cajoling, demanding, pleading, and from time to time I won a brief respite for her, and I suppose for him.

On the few occasions she was permitted to come and stay for a weekend – Marie and I were living together by then – we worked hard to convince her she'd be safe with us. I even went so far as to suggest we set up home, just the two of us, Mum and me. Even through the haze of dementia, she knew all of this was too little too late. They were locked together according to their vows and in a bond none of us could really fathom. I remember one time when she was staying with us and we'd said everything we could say, she asked in a small voice if she could please phone him. She didn't like the idea of his being alone.

My mother may have been his prime victim, but she could also be his protector. Sometimes she would tell me quite firmly to leave things alone. She told me that anything I did would only make him worse, and that if I wanted to help, I should be nice to him. When my sister began to upbraid him for his actions, my mother told her not to interfere with her marriage, and did so with uncharacteristic anger, leaving my sister upset and at a loss. It was simply not in my mother's nature to condemn her own husband to others. She could not do it. There was little we could do to help. I tried many times and failed. And so it went on, for years and years.

It was here in this bungalow that I first organized carers for Mum. My father hated them coming into 'his' home, I suspect because he knew that now there would be eyes on him. The carers came three times a day to look after her, and I began to hope there might at last be some peace of mind. Instead, there were reports of suspicious bruising on Mum's arms, probably from my father's rough handling of her, and when word got back to him, he would no longer allow them to wash her.

Social services attempted to intervene. Mum was put on the 'at risk' register. Brenda, the head of the care agency, tried gentle persuasion over coffee, and went above and beyond to effect some kind of change in him. But the charm he'd used as currency all his life let him get away with it, to begin with. He was always plausible, often fawning, especially with professionals. It became shockingly clear to me that in the eyes of the law, husband and wife have inviolable rights over one another's welfare, and that the law struggles to assert itself in such situations.

I tried to get him counselling. I booked and paid for sessions. I remember waiting in the road outside their bungalow to take him to the therapist. He refused to come out and was stratospherically angry.

My mother would sometimes call me. But only if he was out of the house. We would run through the same script as always: me urging her to leave him, she resisting, the conversation truncated by his return, my mother fearful at the sound of the door opening, a click as the receiver went down, and the sound of the dialling tone.

I need a cigarette, so I open the conservatory doors to the wintry garden. The frost is hardening and the branches are bare. In the darkness beyond, I get the sense that the trees and hedges are unnaturally still. I have to focus.

I am here to sort things out, to find a hospice where my father can see out his last days, to sell the house, clear the debts that have no doubt mounted up and, when the time comes, organize his funeral. The paperwork and the arrangements will take several weeks, maybe a couple of months. My father could last longer, because all that is truly wrong with him is that he has stopped eating and is wasting away. Still, I can return to France and let the professionals at the hospice take care of him. I can visit my mother from time to time, as I've done until now. I can keep my sister, who is six thousand miles away in Canada, up to date, and I can get on with my own life.

But even as I tell myself all this, I know there is a choice. I assisted the authorities in removing my mother from her home because I loved her and wanted to protect her from my father. I still love my mother and I still want to protect her. That hasn't changed. No one will blame me for returning to France and leaving her in the care home, but I don't have to go back. I have no full-time job, no home to pay for, no partner to object, and both my daughters have lives of their own. Phil can build his house without me. The book I am working on could just as well be written here.

Though I have no idea how to go about it or who to ask, or even if it is possible at all, it's clear that when my father dies, I could bring my mother home. I flick my cigarette butt into the darkness and close the doors on the freezing night air. I am free to choose, but no one else can make this decision for me.

▮▮

For three weeks after my return from France, I visited my father in hospital daily, wilting in the warmth of the ward, listening to the sound of his laboured breathing, dabbing ineffectually at his cracked lips with pink foam swabs on white lollipop sticks. He was still eating nothing, but when the doctors suggested force-feeding and the insertion of a nasal tube, my father – in a rare lucid moment – refused point-blank. It was time to call my sister in Canada and tell her she should fly over straight away if she wanted to say her own goodbyes. She booked a flight for the next day and we went to the hospital that evening, but I don't think my father knew we were there.

The next morning, we're walking down the busy corridor of the hospital, jammed with staff and visitors, when a nurse, in something of a panic, asks us to wait before going into our father's room. Moments later, the young doctor in charge skids round the corner, breathless and clearly relieved to have caught us in time. He takes us to one side, away from the crush, and tells us Dad died only minutes before. He says how sorry he is, and suggests we might want some time alone in the room. He says he will wait for us outside.

When the heavy door swings shut behind us, the stillness is unnerving. The air is hot and humid, far too hot for the living. The only sound is the low hum of the inefficient air conditioning. I notice the bed is set strangely high, above waist level, and the pale yellow blanket is tightly tucked around Dad's torso and arms, like a restraint. We step a little closer. His skin has the translucent sheen of old wax. The wisps of grey hair are dry and unkempt. His head is tilted back and his mouth is open, forming a soundless 'O'. I see with a start that his eyelids barely stretch to cover his eyes, probably eased there after death for the sake of the relatives. Us.

The eerie quiet is the most unusual feature of his new incarnation. To hear nothing, not even a breath, is disturbing. He was always a noisy man, and this stiff, contorted figure beneath the blanket is not quite him, instead putting me in mind of those chipped from the ash of Pompeii. Like them, our father has become a stony cast of himself, trapped in a single moment of time. Like them, whatever thought or feeling he had at the end is incomplete, unfinished. I suppose we all die like that, right in the middle of things. At some point, as we parked in the hospital car park and trudged down endless corridors to the ward, he was breathing his last.

'We should have been here,' my sister says through her tears.

I say that most deaths probably happen like this. Unseen, alone. I say there's always something, often something insignificant and arbitrary: a cup of coffee, a breath of fresh air, a cigarette, the desire to sleep. Such simple needs no doubt rob legions of devoted relatives hoping to share the precise moment of death with their loved ones. I say there is no blame.

I can tell I have done little to comfort her, but she knows I'm in a state of shock, not grief. Shock, and relief. Because the whole titanic battle of wills between him and me, all the angst and anger, the bitterness and sheer regret has dissolved into the warm, wet atmosphere of the room, along with his last breath. I didn't expect to be suddenly free of all that. The feeling is heady, disorientating and thrilling.

Twenty-four hours after our father's death, we're on our way to a bulk-buy superstore when we pass some roadkill: a squirrel perhaps, but it's hard to tell; it might once have been a rabbit.

'Oh my God,' my sister cries. 'Poor thing! Do you think it's dead?'

It's clear that the creature, whatever it once was, is now a blood-and-fur inkblot as flat as the tarmac itself. I laugh at the question, and my sister laughs too, though neither of us could really say why. And it helps. If we can court the irreverent now, that's good, because a lot has happened in the last twenty-four hours, and because there's an element of getting to know each other again.

We have lived most of our adult lives on opposite sides of the Atlantic. The last time we spent any real time together, we were still at school. That's forty years ago now, and our childhood memories – my sister caring for birds with broken wings in shoeboxes, coming to me when it was time to bury those that did not survive – are hazy. Like all brothers and sisters, especially those close in age, we bickered, and I teased her mercilessly, but we were a team when it came to Dad and his moods. I remember sitting side by side at the top of the stairs in pyjamas, listening to a row going on below – sometimes a three-way row, with my grandmother shouting as loud as my father, and Mum crying. I would console my sister as best I could.

Our play fights would end in tears or uncontrollable giggles, tickling and wrestling by turns. But we had each other's backs when it came to any outside threat – no one could make my sister cry without reckoning with me – and she, like Mum, knew how to comfort me with small acts of kindness if I was down.

Later, as adolescents, we had our own friends and our lives were more separate – me out on my moped or fixing up cars and listening to Emerson, Lake & Palmer; she reading *Jackie* magazine, posters of David Cassidy and the Partridge Family on the walls of her room, coyly fancying my friends, but too shy to say so.

We are going to the store to buy bin bags, kitchen roll, toilet paper, washing powder, new sheets and towels, and pans to cook with; everything I will need to take care of Mum in her own home.

Because something extraordinary has happened. Neither of us has made a clear decision to bring her home – not in so many words – and yet we both know we are going to do just that. Our father's sudden death means there is no obstacle in our way and no reason not to care for the mother who cared so well for us; no reason not to spend more time with her, to get to know her even, without my father's overbearing presence. Now, it is just her and us. My sister has a career, a partner, a mortgage and lives in Canada, so she will not be on the front line, but she can help with money and moral support.

My children are independent of me. I have no partner and no regular job. You could say my life has stuttered and stalled, and that would also be true. Not many people can make a decision like this – I recognize that – but there is nothing to prevent me becoming Mum's carer if I choose to. And I do. Not just because I put her in the care home or because I promised I would one day bring her home, but because I want to, and because I can. My sister and I have a chance to reach out for a little redemption that might salve the past. The one thing we both know for certain is that we want to grab this gift with both hands.

By the time we park and push one of the oversized shopping trolleys through the sliding doors of the store, we're both high as kites. We should be grieving, facing the dark side. Instead, we're behaving like children, gliding goggle-eyed through a wonderland of surfeit.

We're here for the essentials, but it's hard to resist the luxuries all around us. American barbecues, Italian white goods, the food counters stocked with catering-sized platters of chicken wraps, vast sugar-iced cakes for all occasions, cheeses the size of breeze blocks, olives in buckets, stacks of wine and crates of beer. It's obscene, and glorious. No one has cooked at my parents' bungalow for years. Even before my mother went into the care home, she'd lost the ability to do so. The Parkinson's dementia and the dozens of pills she took each day, one counteracting another, made it impossible for her to work the oven safely. She was often confused, and fainting fits could bring her crashing to the floor at any moment.

Soon the trolley is full to overflowing. At the check-out, it's a shock to find we're spending more than four hundred pounds, but that doesn't dampen our spirits at all. As we pass the security guy on the door, it feels like we're looting in broad daylight, but after a cursory inspection he lets us through, and we're out into the bright February sunshine.

'Are we terrible people?' my sister asks me as we wheel our spoils to the car. 'Shouldn't we be in mourning or something?'

Perhaps we are. But this is also a little epiphany, a new beginning, and it doesn't feel like we're doing wrong. Quite the reverse. Spring is in the air. We've bought masses of material goods, and we're on a mission to liberate our mother.

We unload the car at the bungalow, taking time to put the perishables away but leaving the rest for later. We are keen to head straight to the care home and share our excitement with Mum.

The day room is spacious and high-ceilinged, a sort of orangery. The straight-backed chairs are arranged side by side in U shapes, like an airport departure lounge. There is a large-screen TV on one wall, today showing a sports programme with the sound turned down, as usual. The baby grand piano with its green plastic cover is used as a staging post for tea trays and water jugs and plates of cake. I've never heard it played. To my shame, I've learned to adopt an all-purpose smile for these visits over the last year and a half. Today is different. Today my smile is genuine, because my sister and I are here not with platitudes or patronizing enquiries after our mother's health, but with genuinely good news. No, wonderful news. We've come to tell Mum that her time here is done. Though whether she will recall her home and the promises I've made to take her back there, I can't tell. And I'm conscious there's the not insignificant hurdle of revealing that her release is only possible because her husband of fifty years is dead. How I'm going to tell her that is very much on my mind, but I'll find a way.

This cavernous space is littered with marooned men and women, each a little island of loneliness. We sit either side of her, me on the piano stool, my sister in a resident's chair that happens to be empty. Mum seems alert, though her head is bowed so her chin rests almost on her chest. She looks up, with one eye searching, and seems to recognize us. We ask how she is, but she doesn't reply, distracted by the movement of someone passing by. She doesn't talk very much any more, so my sister chats to her, about the flight over, about the weather, about nothing special, and I have a chance to observe Mum as she is now.

At eighty years of age, her hair is completely grey. But the style is the same as it was when she was a younger woman, swept back and over the ear, collar-length at the back and casually coiffed, a vestige of the 1950s. She has good hair, thick hair, the kind I would have liked to inherit but didn't. Her neat nose has a pale mole on the left nostril that hardly shows, but that I remember from when she was a young woman. Her two top incisors – crowded by the rest of her teeth – are beyond familiar: flared like tiny wings, a feature belonging to her in every era, even those before my time and preserved only in photographs. Those two teeth, so often made prominent by another of her distinguishing features, her easy laugh, are fond childhood memories for me. I haven't seen her laugh in so long. More often I have seen her in tears, especially when it was time for me to leave her yet again, with every visit here.

Her skin is less wrinkled than one might expect at her age, but there is a black patch on her cheek that I am conscious may be a melanoma. I will have to watch for such things if I am to care for her. There's another barely visible mole just under her chin on the right-hand side that I remember produces a white bristle of a hair. She would let me pluck at it with tweezers when I was a boy, rubbing the spot with her finger and giggling, a shared moment that seems remarkably intimate to me now. Her eyebrows were probably plucked hard as a younger woman and are still sparse today. Her eyelashes are full and frame green eyes that have a yellow wash to the whites that they never had when she was young. Nor did her glance dart this way and that, attentive to movement, cautious, even suspicious; at least not as far as I recall.

So much of her has gone, especially since she came to this place. This is a good care home, expensive too, and as far as I can tell the carers are kind and competent. And yet despite their care, Mum walked in here on that first day, leaning on my arm and unsteady, and now she can no longer walk. Sitting for long hours in this chair, her muscles have contracted and atrophied, meaning her legs can no longer straighten. There's little strength left in her arms, and her conscious control of motor functions has all but disappeared. Her ability to communicate is shrinking, and she often has difficulty forming words. She finds it hard to focus, and sometimes forgets she has a visitor at all. That makes me sad, but I wonder if her retreat into what seems to be an alternate reality is not something of a blessing under the circumstances.

Mum was born in 1934 in Alexandria in Egypt, where she grew up alongside her two younger brothers, only visiting England for the first time when she was eighteen. Her father ran a hospital for old warhorses and donkeys that had been worked close to death in the dry heat. She never talked about her youth to me or my sister, but our uncles spoke of a comfortable, even patrician existence, despite the disruptions of the Second World War. There were horses to ride, dogs to protect the property, an English school, and a club where my grandparents gathered with other expats to dance and drink. Mum seems to have taken on much of the responsibility for her two younger brothers, together with a local woman, Badir, who was much loved by the children as a surrogate mother. Badir cooked and cleaned, but to judge by my uncles' stories of their boyhood – jumping from the roof of the two-storey house with an umbrella as a parachute, or using the car radiator as a target for their air rifle – it fell to Mum to try and keep the two boys from serious harm.

When Britain, France and Israel invaded Egypt in what became the Suez Crisis in October 1956, the Egyptian President Nasser ordered the deportation of foreign nationals. The crisis coincided with that first trip my mother made to England with my grandmother. They never went back. My grandfather was put under house arrest and later expelled from the country. The family lost everything they owned and had to start again when they were reunited, with my grandparents both taking jobs at Heathrow Airport. Their daughter and younger son also went on to work in the aviation industry.

My father's upbringing, as one of seven children in Donegal in the west of Ireland, could not have been more different. He would never talk about his youth, and my sister and I never met our paternal grandparents. I got the impression his upbringing was pretty austere and loveless. A few stories trickled out over time, and he and his brothers would talk about the white bread in warm milk that was their staple diet as children, and the one pair of Sunday shoes the boys shared amongst them.

My father's route out of Ireland and poverty was emigration to England as a young man of eighteen to work at Heathrow Airport. It was there that he met my mother. She was a ground hostess, and I still have photographs of her posing in her TWA uniform in the back garden of my grandparents' house at nineteen years of age. There is another picture of her that featured in one of the company's advertising promotions. She looks quite beautiful and very much like Audrey Hepburn, to my eyes anyway. My father was tall and rake-thin, but with fine features and chiselled good looks – shades of Montgomery Clift, perhaps.

They must have made a handsome couple, but my maternal grandmother disapproved. In her eyes, my father was a charming chancer. She still had hopes then that the family might one day recover their losses, though it was not to be, and my father's insistent curiosity over her legal battle to win compensation from the Egyptian government aroused her suspicions that he was a gold-digger too. When at the age of twenty-one, and for the first time ever, Mum defied her mother and married the love of her life, my grandmother declared war. Later on, my father's flirtations and flings with young women at work gave her even more ammunition. Mum had little choice but to defend a man who was often indefensible. She learned to be a peacemaker, assuming the same role when her husband and her son clashed, as we did often. She was always my defender, standing up to him when she could, bringing him down to earth again when the rage had passed.

My mother indulged me. She pretended to believe my stories of sore throats and bad tummies, letting me miss school to spend the day in her bed under the red silk bedcover, leaving Lucozade and ginger biscuits to keep me going. If my father's needs always smothered hers, I wonder now if that overindulged boy did the same.

Still, I have a chance to make it up to her. In becoming Mum's carer, I can face a challenge that defeated and brought out the worst in my father. His story, which for so long obliterated hers, is over. Her story goes on.

While I've been exhuming the past, my mother has tired and is falling asleep in her chair, her eyes rolling, all body strength gone. My sister is trying to keep her upright, but Mum is leaning unnaturally to one side, her neck at an angle. I reach to support her elbow, but the downward pressure of her tiny frame is surprisingly hard to buttress. My sister suggests it might be time to call in some help.

★

Later, when we leave, there is a care worker on either side of my mother. They are pulling her forward in the chair, the better to slip a blue nylon sling behind her torso, which wraps under her arms and fastens across her chest with Velcro. The sling attaches to the two outstretched forks of the hard metal hoist parked and ready to lift her out of the chair and lower her into the waiting wheelchair. I watch every move closely, because in a little while I will be performing this same manoeuvre. By the time we're driving away, the care workers will have wheeled her down the corridor to the bathroom to change her incontinence pad and wipe her clean. At home, all this will be my responsibility.

We look back as we reach the door to the lobby, but can't see Mum for the carers surrounding her and the machinery of the hoist. Soon my sister will return to Canada; this is the last time she will see Mum before she goes. It's not the goodbye she would have wished for, and I can see the effort she is making to hold back tears. We haven't told Mum her husband is dead. The right moment just didn't seem to come along. I tell my sister not to worry. I say I'll handle it. And I will. I have to.

Departure day: my sister is catching a plane for Vancouver and the life she left behind. She's been here only five days and it seems peculiar to be driving her back to the airport so soon.

We're in Dad's red Honda, all charged up and lightly perfumed with the scent of pristine leather. It is cold and raining, so cold the raindrops hitting the car sound like ice. My sister is asking me again, 'Are you really sure about doing this?'

'You'd have to walk otherwise, and with that huge bag … What in God's name is in there?'

'Be serious. You know you can change your mind? No one will blame you. Certainly not me.'

'You worry too much. I'll be fine. We'll be fine.'

We park and take the elevated walkway through to the terminal, heading for a restaurant serving a lot of fried food.

We order two beers and find a table among the motley travellers, most engrossed in their phones or laptops.

'To Dad, I guess …' my sister says, raising her glass.

'Yeah. I'll let you know how things go, probate and so on.'

'And if you need money …'

'Promise.'

I say we'll talk on the phone about Dad's funeral and wake when the autopsy is complete and I have had a chance to organize things. I know she is determined to come back for the ceremony, but I want us to focus on Mum. I say this all feels more like a beginning than an end. This is what we always wanted, time with our mother. It's a dream come true.

'I hope so,' she says as she walks away.

I see her turn to wave as her boarding pass is checked. A moment later, she melts into the crowds funnelling through security.

Driving away from the airport, I'm acutely aware that my sister is not alone in her fears about the future. Objections and reservations have been arriving thick and fast by way of unannounced visits from friends and family, concerned phone calls, and the scepticism of tight-lipped officials.

My dear uncle, for instance. Uncle Pete is Mum's brother and one of my personal heroes, a man with qualities I have always tried hard to emulate. 'Measure twice, cut once' is a favourite phrase of his. He inherited his own father's stoicism, enduring what cannot be changed and changing what must be changed, both usually involving a cup of tea and a toolkit. He cared for his own mother, my maternal grandmother, visiting her daily for fifteen years or more, taking her calls in the middle of the night, risking the wrath of his own partner to meet her often unreasonable demands.

Uncle Pete knows I've been living in France and writing a book, because I sent him a draft only a few months ago. He was encouraging and said it needed work. He worries that I may be well meaning but constitutionally unsuited to self-sacrifice and utterly unprepared for the challenge.

He told me all this, in the nicest possible way, as we sat together at his kitchen table a couple of days ago. He also pushed a thousand pounds in red fifties across the table towards me and said to call him any time. Naturally, I refused the money. He insisted. I promised to pay him back in due course. As I left, he wished me luck and said he had every confidence in me, though in truth I think he's counting in weeks the time it will take for the whole house of cards to collapse around my ears.

Auntie Joyce is not a real auntie at all, but an old friend of my parents who worked at the airport with them. She is in her eighties. I remember her from when

I was a child because she was prone to be outrageous. She had big hair and an even bigger bosom, and her loud, raucous laugh formed the soundtrack to dinner parties at my parents' house, echoing up the stairs to where my sister and I slept, or lay awake and listened intently. So when she arrived unannounced at the bungalow, her grave expression was not what I had expected. She moved cautiously as she came into the house, as if my father might still be there, and only relaxed when we were sitting with a cup of tea in the front room. She said that the last time she was here, my father had slammed the door in her face and told her never to return.

'I hated that man,' she said. 'I know I shouldn't speak ill of the dead, but frankly, good riddance. He treated your mum like a slave all her life.'

None of this was news, and I began to wonder why she had decided to come in person so soon after my call to tell her of Dad's death. There must be more.

'You know I took care of my mother,' she says. 'Well, it nearly killed me, and at the end I had to put her in a home. I couldn't cope, not with the way she behaved, and she didn't even have dementia. She was a nightmare.'

I know she meant well, but the cumulative effect of her words and her obvious distress at recalling her own experiences was doing neither of us any good. I tried to take her back to the old days, when she and my parents were young and worked together, and partied too, but I couldn't shake her mood.

As she was leaving, she said, 'And it ruined me financially.' I waved her off with a sigh of relief.

Only the other day, Brenda from the care agency rang to say she would like to come and see us. I was delighted. I had called her and outlined the plan to bring Mum home, hoping her agency would be able to help me with care, and I thought her visit might be to confirm. I could not have been more wrong. Brenda's case was simple. Mum's needs, she said, were way beyond the skills of her own carers, and to be frank, she thought I had no idea what I was letting myself in for. She brought along her head of operations, a grand title for a woman short in stature, who backed up her boss with nods and emphatic one-liners such as 'That's true' and 'It's better to face facts now rather than find out later.'

But it was the care home manager who had the most surprising reaction of all.

'No one's ever done this,' she said, when I told her I intended to take Mum home. She asked if I had checked with social services, and I told her I had. She seemed somehow personally affronted by the proposal and unsure what to say next.

'Is there any paperwork you and I should be doing?' I asked.

'I'll have to check. I'll let you know by email.'

After our meeting, I went to the day room to sit with Mum for a while. Stella, the care home's hairdresser, walked by and stopped to chat. I told her about my meeting with the manager.

'Doesn't surprise me,' she said, leaning towards me conspiratorially. 'The only way anyone gets out of here is in a box.'

Now my sister is safely in the air, I confess that while I detect nothing but goodwill and genuine concern behind these entreaties, I am a little unnerved. Not only is the plan to take Mum out of the care home and look after her myself clearly suspect in some people's eyes, but it seems I am personally suspect, too. My motives and my ability to cope with the pressures of becoming a carer have been brought into question, and I have yet to receive a vote of confidence from anyone.

When my ex-wife and I were breaking up, she said to me: 'You have an inordinate need for personal freedom.'

Note the 'inordinate'. The dictionary offers these synonyms by way of definition: *improper, immoderate or excessive*. This observation, like the others, clearly implies that becoming a carer for my mother might not play to my strengths. Perhaps I lack the temperament to survive domestic captivity. Perhaps I'll run for the hills.

I've done it before. Running away, that is. Twice, in fact, and both times to France, once after my divorce and again six months after Mum had gone into the care home. To be fair to myself, the first time I gave in to wanderlust was long after the marriage had broken down and my wife and I had separated. My first reaction to the news that she had feelings for her business partner was not to run for the hills, but rather to dig my heels in and fight against the inevitable every step of the way. Which is not to say the new love caused the death of the old, any more than my inordinate need for personal freedom was the reason for my wife's falling out of love with me.

We had gone out together briefly at school, an institution run by a Catholic order of priests and nuns known as the Salesians, milder than the Jesuits, though with a similar penchant for discipline and sometimes corporal punishment. At seventeen, I was painfully shy, but with attitude. I let my greasy hair snake over my neck and low on the forehead, and I kept my hands permanently in my pockets. My tie hung like a noose, shirt collar unbuttoned, and the steel quarters on the heels of my oxblood leather shoes chinked and clunked as I walked, feet splayed, eyes down. My worn barathea school blazer – thick wool blazers were decidedly uncool – had silvered buttons showing the brass beneath. I wore the collar up, tucked under my hair, until I was told to tidy myself by one of the brothers or sisters of the order, who were also our teachers.

I may have lacked something in the way of style, but what I did have – for the first time in my life – were feelings. Thumping heart, sweaty palms, sleepless nights, the whole shooting match – not for my future wife, but for the half-Italian beauty who sat opposite me in our A-level English class.

I distanced myself from the other lads at school and signed up for a correspondence course in English literature designed to fill in some fairly sizeable gaps in my knowledge. My parents were pleased and surprised. I cultivated the subdued, rather sorrowful air I imagined characterized all artists and writers, and sat long into the night on my bed, poring over Milton beneath a poster of an angry Old Testament God by Blake, imagining what it might be like to touch the girl of my dreams.

I stopped spending the money I earned stacking shelves at weekends on obscure progressive rock albums and began to save. My seventeenth birthday was around the corner, I was still a virgin, and I would soon be able to drive, legally. You couldn't drive and be a virgin. You just couldn't.

Then I saw it in the local paper: an abandoned restoration job, lacking an engine. It was not a beast, but it was a sports car and it was the right price. The guy wanted £120. With my two petrol-head buddies in tow, I hunted about the scrapyards and came up with an engine for fifteen quid that would slot in nicely, with one or two home-made modifications. Two weeks before my seventeenth birthday, the car was ready and so was I.

I took the test on my birthday and passed, first time. I was a man (not a boy) with a mission, driven by the power of love and a rusty 1200cc Triumph Spitfire. I drove to school the next day through pouring rain, the torn soft-top leaking from so many places it looked like I had swum there. When I got there, I discovered my Italian beauty was not even at school, and wouldn't be there for weeks to come. She had glandular fever. The kissing disease. I was outraged.

In deep despair, I started giving another girl in my English class a lift home occasionally – a girl I would one day marry. She was good company. We laughed together and chatted easily. We went out for three weeks, until the Italian beauty recovered and danced with me at the Ottershaw disco. It was she I drove home that night, much to my shame.

Ten years later, having apparently forgiven me, my wife-to-be and I met for a drink in London. I was working as a journalist and she as an architect. I was tired and bruised, having lost the Italian beauty to her future husband after a decade as a couple, entirely through my own negligence. I had left her and gone to do an MA in America, finally succumbing to the allure of that heathen land and making an early bid for personal freedom, something that would later become a habit.

My wife-to-be had a long-term boyfriend. She was keen to settle down, but he was not. We met a few times as friends, and when she complained again about her boyfriend's lack of commitment, I said, 'Just be done with it and marry me.' I was joking and she laughed, but the more often we met, the more I began to recognize that I might feel something more than friendship for her. I had money to spare with a journalist's expense account, and dashing around town in cabs, eating in restaurants and buying flowers on impulse became part of our relationship. I knew better than to put her under any pressure, as she clearly still felt a lot for her boyfriend, so I made sure our time together was easy and full of fun, though in truth I was courting her without ever admitting it.

We got married two years later. We travelled in India and Malaysia for six months before going on to have our two children. We seldom argued and we worked hard together to build a life and nurture our kids. And we were good at it. Some people called us 'the perfect couple'. But one day – I don't know when exactly – she realized she had made the fatal error of mistaking friendship for love. After thirteen years as a dutiful wife and mother to two children, she wanted more from life, and especially from love.

By the time of the break-up, we were living in the countryside. I'd become a television producer and company director and was commuting to London every day, but with the divorce, I gave that up. I took a job working in a local off-licence so I could be at the school gates every bit as often as my soon-to-be ex-wife. For a long time, we shared the same house. That was hard. Later, when we lived apart, our two daughters spent their time with us equally. I became a very bad painter-decorator – setting fire to one house and flooding another – but it was not just my wife who was undergoing a profound change in her life. I had loved every moment of being a father. I was even good at it, much to my own surprise. I was a single parent for half the time at least, and I had stumbled across my métier. In losing my wife's love, I had forged the strongest of bonds with my daughters, hour upon hour, day by long day, through the weeks and months and even years of the break-up. My weaknesses as a man, the very qualities that had helped to drive my wife to distraction – the juvenile need to play, the notion that you could live on a boat and fish off the side for food, the idea that sticking at anything meant a lifetime of drabness and boredom; in short, my inability to grow up – had all at once become my strength. I was fluent in child.

We made our own burgers and added toppings of cheese and pickle and tomato and lettuce and sauces galore. When supper was done and there was no ice cream in the freezer and no money in the bank, the three of us would scour the house together, gathering up loose change lurking under beds and in pockets, then head to the petrol station and choose three of the most extravagant ice creams on sticks we could find. We watched the classic children's films, *The Jungle Book*, *The Little Mermaid, Beauty and the Beast*, but we had our own particular favourites like *Shane, To Kill a Mockingbird* and *Some Like It Hot*, films we had to buy because we watched them so many times. When the weather was warm, we would drive to the beach after school, stopping to pick up French bread and cheese, or half a ready-roasted chicken, and cans of cider and lemonade. We swam in the early-evening light and drove home as the sun went down, the girls dozing and content, wrapped in towels with sand in their hair and between their toes. We loved the beach and the sea so much that I bought a VW camper van with money borrowed, rather cheekily, from my generous ex, to live the dream. I took the girls, and our newly acquired springer spaniel – shared, naturally – surfing in Cornwall in the summers, and we went there for winter breaks too. We would rent a house with friends and don wetsuits to charge into the freezing ocean at Polzeath, just for the devilment.

Together, we had time, that most priceless of commodities: time to share a myriad of experiences and time to get to know each other. There was even enough time for me to begin to get to know myself. I began to feel like a better person, like I was maturing by spending time with my children, very possibly the only authentic way for a man like me to grow up.

We were lucky. I was lucky. Despite all the anger and pain, there was no wrangling over custody, no battles over money, and our daughters spent equal time with their mother and their father. We shared Christmas as a family, and still do to this day.

So whatever the doubters may say about this plan to care for my mother, whatever aspersions are cast my way, whatever doubts I may have about myself, there is at least the knowledge that I have grown into a proper dad. That alone offers me a glimmer of hope in my bid to become my mother's carer.

IV

I had forgotten how grey England can be, and how long the grey lasts, day after endless day. I miss the blue skies of the south of France. Already my year there feels like a long-ago vacation, pictures in a brochure of another life.

A week since my sister left, and I'm at the bungalow making last attempts to contact those who should be informed of my father's passing. I've gone through every old address book I could find, all his email addresses, even a Christmas card list I found, and though I am sure to have missed important people, I have tried to be diligent. Probate is chugging along, or so the solicitor assures me. I spend countless hours approaching home care agencies and being turned down with various excuses when they hear that Mum has to be hoisted from wheelchair to bed, and that she is incontinent and unable to feed herself.

When I tell them I want to be fully involved with her personal care, working alongside the carers, the response is even cooler. I'm told that, by law, agencies cannot work with anyone who is untrained. I say I am quite prepared to learn manual handling techniques and will be responsible for everything else, from feeding to medications, but it does little to persuade them I can be trusted. I can't help wondering if my gender only adds to their suspicions.

My sister and I did a lot while she was here, but there is more to do. We've hired a solicitor, filled in various forms, and faced the finances, too, only to find a black hole where there should be money to spare. If it was ever there, it isn't now. Judging by the bank statements, it looks to me like a quarter of a million pounds has gone out the door, most of it on care and all of it in just the last couple of years. My father could not cope with his affairs and refused to let any family member help, but it is patently clear from letters received that my mother's care home is owed £27,000, and they are anxious to recover the money. I will need to address the debt with their head office in order to negotiate my mother's release. Not that they can hold her hostage; that would be unseemly. The rest of the paperwork is a mess, but I can attack that over the weeks to come.

We are waiting for the autopsy. The cause of my father's death at the age of eighty is listed as pneumonia, but to my mind, his decision not to eat and his desire to die were the real causes, and no treatment the doctors could offer could have cured the condition. He had always suspected that 'the Big C', as he called it, was waiting for him, though he had never had any serious illnesses, and the only operation he ever had was two weeks before his death, when he had his big toe amputated. It had become necrotic – the flesh had blackened and died – through having the weight of blankets pressing down on it for so long. His life savings were gone. Everything he'd worked so hard to accumulate had seeped away in his last years, along with his will to live. That was why he had taken to his bed, refusing to eat and shrivelling from a big man of six foot two and thirteen stone to a wizened stick less than six stone in weight. The only way he knew to carry on his war with an unjust world was to turn the assault on his own body. An autopsy can't tell you those things.

'What are you doing here?' Mum says, as I pull up a chair and sit in front of her at the care home.

She's smiling, as if relishing my surprise. Her head is bowed as usual, but with one eyebrow raised as if to say 'gotcha'. I'm taken aback as always by these sudden flashes of lucidity.

Articulate, engaged, aware, funny, even cheeky: these are qualities in her I forget to remember. They are rarely apparent now, and before she was ill, my father quashed them. I always stumble and trip over myself to pack in whatever meaningful communication we can before something or someone, imaginary or real, distracts her from the present and from my presence.

I've talked to her about bringing her home, but I have shied away from mentioning Dad's death. I have no real notion of how she will take the news. I have considered the possibility of saying nothing at all, or of waiting until she is at home, but neither feels right, so I've elected to make her mood and her lucidity the deciding factors.

Which means today might just be the day. We are seated in the conservatory. Light and airy, it is usually deserted at this time of day, and we can lunch together away from the other residents with a chance to talk openly.

My plan is to say that when my sister and I saw Dad in hospital, his last wish was that Mum should come home and take care of the bungalow, just as he had done in her absence. Not a very sophisticated opening gambit, I know, but my hope is that in taking baby steps towards the question of mortality, I can soften the news of Dad's death.

I sit in a bamboo-framed armchair next to Mum's wheelchair, with a hospital table in front of us. Lunch turns out to be an unappetizing grey mince in gravy with mashed potato. I don't spend long trying to spoon it into her mouth before we move on to treacle tart and custard, which goes down well. I make a promise to myself that good home cooking will be the signature note of my care.

I take a breath. The time feels right.

'Mum, you remember I said we'd take you home?'

She smiles and is apparently listening. But she says nothing.

'Well, the day is coming very soon. Is that okay?'

She doesn't speak and there's no change to her expression.

'Because that's what Dad wanted. And I hope that's what you want. Is it?'

The carer returns to take the tray and catches Mum's attention. Movement, particularly if it comes unexpectedly and takes human form, will often generate a quick response in her, and she'll follow whoever it is with an alert interest.

'Mum?'

I take her hand. She looks down to see what the touch is all about and her eyes trace a line over the cardigan, up my arm to my shoulder and face. She's back.

'I was saying, we're going to get you home soon, though I have to warn you, it'll be me taking care of you. What do you think of them apples?'

She starts to cough. As her vocal cords prepared to go to work, a bit of phlegm lazing around in her throat shifted and has caused a blockage. I'll find out in the months to come that dysphagia – disruption to the swallowing process – will be one of my greatest enemies and, though a mechanical complaint, life-threatening to my mother. She's leaning far enough forward in the chair for me to rub her back in little circular motions I can't imagine do much to ease her coughing, but that serve to make me feel better. I tap a couple of times with the flat of my hand, the way you do when someone is choking, and reach for the orange squash in a plastic cup on the table. She raises her own hand to the cup and takes a surprisingly firm grip of one of my fingers as she sips the liquid. I wait for her to recover. Then, as her breathing returns to normal, I put the cup down and take her hand in mine.

'Mum, I need to talk to you about Dad. You know he was in the hospital?'

'Where is he now?' she asks unexpectedly, and I'm confounded.

Come on, I tell myself. You've got her attention. Answer the question. Is he still in the hospital or not? Technically I suppose he is, in so far as his body is in the morgue and the morgue is in the hospital. Can I be economical with the truth? But if I say he's in hospital, doesn't that imply that he's still alive? Or should I take a run at this and explain that he died more than a week ago now?

I find myself sidestepping the question altogether.

'Dad was ill, you remember? He couldn't be at home

alone without you, and so he went to the hospital. They looked after him there. He told me I should take you home, and that's what I'm going to do. He died happy to know that you'd be safe with me.'

I'm waiting for a reaction that isn't going to come. I can't tell if the news is either not news at all – they hadn't seen each other for more than a year, since he took to his bed – or the kind of news that simply doesn't compute any more. Either way, the information has been put aside, and I haven't the heart to drive it home except in the weediest of words.

'Are you all right?' I ask. Nada.

'He was happy at the end,' I say. A lie.

'I was with him.' A detestable lie. 'And Sis too.'

I am completely without honour, but it just doesn't seem to matter any more. I can say whatever I like. So I do.

'He loved you very much,' I say.

And suddenly, I wonder. Because it occurs to me that I might just have spoken a truth, despite myself.

Talking to Mum today, recalling my father and their relationship, has revived questions concerning the nature of love that I began asking myself in earnest when my wife and I were breaking up, and have been asking ever since.

It is all too easy to assume love is always a good thing, worth seeking and preserving when you find it, or when it finds you. But does it follow that love is a state where you have only the best interests of the other at heart? Where what is given is given freely, with no expectation of reward or even recognition?

Perhaps love is not selfless at all, but the opposite. More like a pact, a service agreement, or a contract. You meet my needs and I'll meet yours, utterly different and even contradictory as those needs may be. This person is outgoing, the other introverted, for instance, thus creating a relationship of two individuals who counterpoint one another in a harmony of opposites. What we call love is not always, or even often, a perfectly balanced set of shiny brass scales with two little heaps of the same gold dust in either saucer. More often, the trade-off is for goods of an entirely different nature and far from equal.

We may want to think about love in terms of right and wrong, black and white, but things tend to be a little more grey when you're on the inside looking out. Romantic love is a very private affair, because let's face it, not all of our most intimate emotional needs are publicly acceptable. Closed doors are there for a reason. Far too easily we condemn relationships as being unusual or unethical when they are perfectly acceptable to those in love. Is there such a thing as good love and bad love?

I have to suppose my mother put up with my father's appalling behaviour because she loved him, for better or worse. I think my father loved my mother very much in return, even as he made her life hell. When I took her away for weekends to give them both a break, he pined and fretted. He could not bear to be away from her. When she went into the care home, he stopped eating. When she didn't come home, he died. Is that a kind of love? Or was his so-called love an illegitimate need, a stifling instinct for control, anathema to the rest of us, though not, it seems, to my mother?

Stranger still than his love for her, if indeed that's what it was, is her love for him. She stood by him for fifty years. She fought off attempts to rescue her and defended him against those who criticized. She loved him, despite it all. And that, however much I might wish it different, is plain fact.

It is almost three weeks after Dad's death, and I've only just been notified that the autopsy is complete. His body is now available to be collected from the hospital, and I have presented the death certificate at the Registrar of Births, Deaths and Marriages, to register his death formally. All this officialdom is new to me, and it's an odd experience, but I'm working my way through it step by step, and still visiting Mum while trying to keep up with the protocols of probate.

I should have been ready for this day, and I have tried to prepare. I have investigated a few local funeral directors, but now the time has come, I'm still not sure of the best thing to do. The offering from the Co-op includes what they call an 'ambulance' from hospital mortuary to their premises, a wooden coffin – from sustainable wood, they say – and a hearse with driver and four pallbearers. All this for a little over two and a half thousand pounds, excluding the costs of a priest to officiate, and the hire of facilities such as the chapel in which to hold a service, a venue for the wake and the cost of catering.

I didn't want to say that, for a variety of reasons, it was likely the pallbearers would outnumber the mourners, nor did I want to appear parsimonious in honouring my dead parent with due care and conscience. But neither could I see the rationale in following form merely through fear of offending custom. I decide to call my sister in Canada. When she was here, we had talked about the options but came to no conclusions. She has a cool head and will know the best thing to do.

'We should go for a cremation,' she says. 'That way we can figure out the funeral arrangements later. I can't come over again now, I've only just got back to work. We don't know who else to invite, other than family, and there's not many of them left. Even Mum can't be there.'

'So you think it's best we wait to hold a funeral?'

'Have you heard of a celebration of life?'

'I've heard the term.'

'They do it over here all the time. No church service, just friends and family gathering together. We could do that.'

'So what do I do now?'

'Arrange the cremation. You've got a lot on your plate; I'll do some research and send you whatever I can find.'

Sis sends me links to five websites, and we decide to go with the company that is most affordable and can carry out a simple cremation. She also transfers the money to my account, as I have run out of cash and still cannot access my parents' accounts, because they are locked until probate is complete. All of which makes me wonder how other people deal with these situations.

I've chosen a cremation service. I've checked the company out online and I've spoken to the managing director. He tells me that many people these days opt for non-traditional ways to mark the passing of their loved ones, and that a celebration of life is among the most popular.

I take a day to think things over and double-check the company's reviews, which are all good. I begin to look into what a celebration of life might be like, and I find there are as many variations on the theme as there are individuals. The whole idea is that it should reflect the unique qualities of the person whose life is being celebrated. That starts me thinking. Dad's first choice of venue might be the golf club, but a close second would be his garden, with a barbecue maybe. He loved to barbecue. And that in turn makes me think about Mum's homecoming, which is only a month away now. If the weather is kind – and I know that's a risk – we might be able to combine the two celebrations into one. My sister could be there, and that's really important for all of us, but I would also have time to search out friends and family and invite them too.

I call my sister again, and she is all for it. I send off the paperwork, and alert the morgue that I have arranged for Dad's body to be collected.

While the cremation service I chose was an affordable option, it may not prove to have been the best. Two weeks after my father's body was collected from the hospital, I am still waiting. My calls are not being returned, and nor are my father's ashes.

This unexpected development could prove embarrassing, as I've managed to get a guest list together and am currently sending out the invitations to the celebration of life, now just five weeks away. And though of course nobody is anticipating seeing my father in person, having his ashes to hand would be expected.

Having him there in some tangible way is all the more important given the strong Irish contingent on the guest list. Dad led many of them to believe I was a serious menace to the family, and I need no help adding to that impression. This will not look good to them.

I phone the hospital morgue just to be sure my father has been picked up. He has. I ask if they have a mobile number in their paperwork that might help me track his progress across country towards the crematorium, ninety miles from the hospital. They don't. I ask if this situation has arisen before now. It hasn't, but then the woman on the other end says they almost always know the funeral directors who take bodies for burial or cremation, because they tend to be local. I feel chastised. I ask if I'm the first to use this company. She tells me I am.

A week later, all I have to show for my time are more unreturned phone calls. My sister wants to know if it's possible Dad's been dumped somewhere, and she'd really like to know why I thought paying the full amount up front was a sensible thing to do. I decide to call the local police in the town where the cremation service is located.

The policewoman at the other end of the phone is kind and patient. She listens as I stumble through an explanation of how I chanced upon the company even though I live so far away, but when I ask if she has any knowledge of it or its activities, she says no. It's something of a relief that I haven't been had by a nationwide scam, but does little to resolve the current issue as to where he's got to.

I'm waiting for her to suggest sending a squad car to the premises with a couple of beefy officers and one of those pipe things they use to break down doors. She proposes instead that I write a letter to the company and send it registered post, which seems quaint and potentially ineffective. She asks me to call back if I get no joy from the letter, after which I'm pretty sure she retires to the staff room to relay the story to her colleagues as another example of why police officers should be paid on a par with psychiatrists, and why policing ain't what it used to be.

Eventually, of course, my father came home. I finally got the young boss of the company on the phone by filling in the enquiry form on the website and claiming to be a potential new client in need of a call back. When I told him I'd been in touch with the police, he had the ashes with me in no time.

A fabulously skinny young man handed Dad over in a green plastic urn with a formal bow and a couple of quick backward steps, gingerly offering me the cremation certificate in a buff envelope, as if expecting trouble. He'd had a long drive that morning only to drive all the way back when his duty was discharged, and I suppose he was keen to get on. I thanked him and waited at the front door with Dad under my arm as the young man turned his van around.

A few hours later, when the time difference allowed, I called my sister in Canada and told her the wanderer had returned.

'I am so relieved,' she said. 'I feel like celebrating now, but it's only eight o'clock in the morning here. Have one for me.'

SPRING

V

I'm getting used to putting on a sweater and even a coat before I venture from the bungalow. I'm short of warm clothing, having packed a single carry-on bag when I flew in, but the charity shops are providing me with anything I lack. Still, I feel the cold, more so since I was in France, and dressing inappropriately does not help. There, I wore shorts all year round. Here, I try to do the same through habit and for reasons of comfort, but with the outside temperatures still low some days, I think I must cut an odd figure in public. I can only hope the assumption is that I have gone straight from the gym to the shops, and don't look quite as foolhardy as in fact I am.

And I'm getting up earlier to take full advantage of any available daylight, as the days feel very short. There's paperwork to do at my father's desk each day – probate is sluggish, the tax authorities seem not to have understood that he has passed away and are chasing for his tax return, and the accountant is trying to track savings in a bond – but I try to get outside when I can, if only to shop or do chores. With no money of my own, I'm very careful what I spend. My sister is digging into her savings while we wait for probate, but that puts a strain on her finances. Uncle Pete's money is a help, but I'm still embarrassed to have said yes, and I'm hoping to preserve most of it until probate clears and I can access my father's bank account.

My latest 'to do' list includes the following:

- Take will to new solicitor handling probate
- Arrange care inspection visit with Dot
- Clean out cupboards in Dad's room
- Register with GP (Mum and me)
- Talk to the occupational therapist re bed etc.
- Make list of medications – ask care home

No deadlines are indicated, but overambition leads me to try to do everything on the list in one day. An early start helps, and soon after eight o'clock I am driving to our solicitor's office with the original of my father's will. After much detective work, I have finally retrieved it from my father's solicitor, who does not handle probate work and who, at first, amid obfuscations and Dickensian delays, denied holding the will at all.

I am back at the bungalow by half past nine. Dot, a manager at the only care agency that has agreed to consider working with us, is due at midday. She has already visited the care home to assess Mum's needs and has told me by phone that her agency will be able to take us on, subject only to a quick assessment at the bungalow and a contract, which is marvellous, because several agencies have turned me down and I'm running out of options. There is just time for me to get to the local GP surgery to register both Mum and myself.

At the surgery, I queue for ten minutes only for the receptionist to tell me I cannot register Mum until she is released from the care home, because she will no doubt be under the care of another surgery while a resident there. She asks for the name of the doctor or surgery and I confess I don't know. Once Mum is back in her own home, I should return, making sure to bring her medical card and NHS number. The receptionist hands me back the card with the number emblazoned in purple, and I thank her for the advice.

I get home from the surgery to find Dot sitting in her four-wheel drive outside. She is twenty minutes early, but still I wonder if I've got the time wrong and should apologize. I peer through her car window, only to find she is on her phone. She is trying to tell me she won't be long with hand gestures. I make a drinking-from-a-mug sign and get a thumbs-up.

★

Coffees in hand, we sit in the kitchen to do the paperwork. Dot has looked around the house and said the hospital bed, when it arrives, would be best in the dining room or my father's room, so the carers can access both sides of it. She is ticking boxes as we go.

'So we're looking at a standing hoist, that's right, isn't it?'

'Um, yes, a standing hoist, I'm pretty sure. Like the care home.'

'Good, so, next of kin, other than you, obviously?' She laughs. I tell her my sister lives in Canada.

There are more questions and answers – religious affiliation, doctor's name, public liability, medication disclaimer, emergency numbers in case of hospitalization – and at last Dot hands me a copy of the contract to read over.

'I'm sure it's all fine. Shall I just sign?'

'If you like, yes, it's all standard, though just so you know, it's seven days' written notice to cancel the service, forty-eight hours for individual care calls, just give us a ring and then there's no charge, like if you're going out for the day …'

Her optimism is heartening.

'… all our carers are CRB-checked and, oh, if you can get an incontinence form from the surgery, did they mention that?'

I thank her and hand back the signed contract. I feel a little overwhelmed by Dot and the new things I should add to my lists, leading me to ask a rather pathetic question.

'Do other people do this? Take a relative out of a care home, I mean?'

'Not really, no, it's a bit unusual. You get plenty going in, but not coming back out, no. Still, if it doesn't work out, at least you can say you tried, can't you?'

She checks her phone.

'I should get going. I'm going out tonight, and I'm running late as it is ...'

I visit Mum every day in order to keep the lines of communication open. I want to make sure she has a chance to get used to the idea of coming home, and to get used to me again, before we're together every day. This is a big thing we're doing, and potentially traumatic for her after so long at the care home. I still can't tell how she is responding to Dad's death, or even if she knows it has happened at all.

I kiss her on the forehead and sit beside her in an empty chair. I've timed my visit well – I get a cup of tea of my own, and a slice of cake. It's been a busy day, but I have to remind myself to relax and to appreciate that all this – the residents, the carers, the home itself – will soon be consigned to memory.

Now that I'm here every day, I know most of the regular carers. They constitute an international brigade, from Romania, Poland, Spain, Zimbabwe, among other countries. Gizela is a young grandmother in her fifties. She is from Poland and has been working in the UK for several years now. She came originally for a few months, and only in order to earn enough money for a new fridge and cooker, or so she told me rather ruefully. She is still here because her extended family, including a husband, a son, a daughter who is newly married and three grandchildren, have come to rely completely on the money she earns, though it can't be more than a few hundred pounds a week, less after she pays rent and living expenses. She tells me she lives alone in a bedsit a few miles from work. Then there's a tall man who looks like an athlete, because that's exactly what he is, or was, in Zimbabwe. He has a wife and two small children, and the money he earns keeps them afloat in a way that athletics could not. His name is Clayt, with a 't', and I notice that whenever the wall TV is on and showing sport, he will slow his easy lope past the screen, pausing to watch even though the sound is invariably turned down. I've talked about Mum being marooned here and my being marooned at the bungalow. I wonder if Gizela and Clayt feel marooned. Do they resent the inequalities and the mad economics that take them so far from home and bring them here to care for us? I haven't dared to ask.

Many of the residents are now familiar faces, too. Most are in the same spot every day, because they are unable to move independently, but Theresa is a notable exception, always on the move, taking tentative steps in this direction or that, wringing her hands together as she approaches carers and visitors, asking in her lilting Irish accent what she should be doing. I always look for her when I arrive, and always feel relieved when I spot her, neatly turned out in a tweed skirt, her white hair held in a tidy bob with hairpins, squinting over glasses that sit at the very tip of her nose.

If it is a carer she has buttonholed, she'll be told it's almost time for lunch or tea, and that she shouldn't worry. If it's a visitor, there's often an element of comedy as the poor unfortunate stumbles to explain that they're simply here to see a relative. Theresa is politely persistent, often leading the visitor to look around for help and join her in calling for a nurse. I don't always jump in to rescue the situation.

I didn't engage much with Theresa to start with, other than to be polite, because I thought there was little chance of any meaningful communication between us, beyond my fielding of her urgent entreaties. I only recently discovered that she can converse cogently and even colourfully about anything at all: the other residents, her long years as a nurse in London, and her home town in Ireland, despite not having been back in more than fifty years. Talking about her life seems to alleviate her anxiety for a time, and the quirk of behaviour that forces her to wonder what she should be doing. One of the carers recently told me Theresa is one hundred and two years old.

I should not have favourites, but I do. My second favourite after Theresa is Ruby, who sits some distance away in a wheelchair. Ruby has bright eyes and a habit of sucking in air through her teeth with a wet sound, as if she's salivating. Her son – we nod at each other when our visits happen to coincide – is a commercial pilot. He appears a bit stiff, dour even – possibly ex-military, I think to myself – and the polar opposite of his mother, who seems positively excited by life. Often, when I arrive to visit Mum, I'll pass close to Ruby as I take one of the spare chairs stacked against the wall. Early on, she smiled and said a coquettish 'Halloo!' that caught me entirely by surprise, her cut-glass accent purring into an appreciative 'My, you're a big boy' that quite made me blush at the time and still gives me pleasure now. It's not often as a man that you get chatted up.

There are fewer male residents, and finding themselves so outnumbered, they seem to shrink from public view, as if they might be embarrassed to be here. I once had occasion to talk with a man who gave some credence to the idea. It was odd. I was having tea with Mum when he beckoned me over to where he was sitting in a wheelchair, away from the other residents. I took him to be a visitor, an impression only strengthened when he asked me to lean closer and said conspiratorially, 'Rather depressing here, isn't it? Poor old buggers.'

I didn't feel comfortable agreeing, not in so many words, though I couldn't help but have sympathy with the sentiment. We made small talk for a few minutes until he caught the attention of a passing carer.

'I want a cigarette,' he said imperiously.

The carer smiled indulgently. 'You know you can't smoke in here.'

'Then take me outside.'

'No smoking outside, it's bad for you.'

'Oh for God's sake.'

His irritation was palpable. I went back to Mum as the argument continued.

'It's just a bloody cigarette …'

'Supper soon, eh?'

'I don't want supper, I want a cigarette.'

'If we go now, we'll get a good place.'

'I'm not bloody hungry,' I heard him say as the carer began to wheel him away towards the dining room.

Though it is spring, the afternoons are still short and it is dark by six thirty, so I put the lights on when I get home. I miss the sun at this time of year especially, when the skies are so often cloudy.

But it's been a good day, with everything on the list achieved bar the cupboard cleaning, and that can wait. But Ruby, and cigarette man, and Theresa linger in my mind this evening, perhaps because I won't be seeing them for very much longer.

They share something in common, beyond ending their days in the care home, though I don't know what name to give it. The German philosopher Schopenhauer might have called Theresa's need to be useful, Ruby's need to flirt and even cigarette man's desire to smoke 'the will to live', though that might seem contradictory given the health advice on cigarette packets. Freud talked about 'the pleasure principle', and Viktor Frankl, who spent time in a Nazi concentration camp, thought the basic drive of human beings was the creation of meaning in our lives. Likely as not, a combination of these impulses impels us on in life, into old age and indeed all the way to the end.

Ruby wasn't flirting today. She was asleep when I arrived, and though I didn't notice her go, she was no longer in the day room by the time I left. Theresa was sitting behind Magda at the reception desk, waiting for any task she might help with. I haven't seen cigarette man for more than a year now, and I have to suppose he may have died, no doubt deprived of the traditional last cigarette, though I prefer to think he might be sitting in the garden, contentedly surrounded by a little fog of his own making.

When Mum is home again, I will encourage her to play and to tease, though perhaps not to smoke. Her will to live is what has kept her going in the care home, and taking her from that busy, if hermetic, environment to the smaller, more isolated bungalow could potentially prove harmful to her, unless we make the most of every day. In practical terms, wind, rain, takeaways, and a gin and tonic in the evenings.

Things will be different here. Better. And life will go on, for me and for Mum. Not just because it's the right thing to do, but because it's what I would want for myself. I decided I would take this on only if I thought I could do it with some kind of grace, do it lightly and with good humour. What I didn't say, but what I'm beginning to feel very strongly, is that in order to be a decent carer, in order to give Mum a life that is full and fulfilling, I must also have a life of my own. The point is to bring her back into the world. And life as lived means laughter, tears, obstacles, challenges and even risk, but especially love – for both of us.

And yet here I am, marooned in the bungalow, just as Mum is marooned in the care home, just as Gizela and Clayt are marooned in a country not their own. I am well aware that I am the designated giver and she the receiver. There are barriers between her inner world and mine. I know she sleeps a lot and talks very little and I have to keep my expectations low. That's the deal, and I'm fine with it, but already I can sense that the hours of caring are likely to be less onerous than the hours of waiting to care. I know this feeling of isolation is unlikely to go away when Mum and I are alone here together. There is always the phone, but empty evenings will be common, even constant.

The question is, what can I do?

VI

The last time I looked for love, I had to travel a thousand kilometres to find someone, and it only took twenty-four hours to lose her.

It was the second time I ran away to France, a year ago now, after Marie and I hit the buffers. My mother was in the care home and I had finally cut all contact with my father. With the weather in England at its most flat and grey, a road trip south and a new start seemed not only attractive, but the only choice open.

My elder daughter was to be my travelling companion. It was early March when we set off, by chance almost exactly a year ago today. My younger daughter was then twenty years old. She was studying drama at university and enjoying life. The elder, at twenty-four, needed a fresh start as much as her father did. She'd graduated the summer before and gone through the usual excoriating process we call 'getting a job after university'. Fluent in

French and Spanish, she was thinking about a further degree at a French university. We both had reasons to get away, and the chance of doing so together was irresistible.

Four hours' drive from the ferry port at Dieppe, and we were climbing towards the bleak plateau of the Massif and into the volcanic region of the Auvergne. Cone-shaped volcanoes, disused chimneys of a subterranean world, rose stark against a white winter sun. We stopped once for coffee and a cigarette, and once to fill up with petrol. Another three hours and we were winding down the hairpins of the steeper southern edge of the plateau soon after the Millau bridge. Rust-red pantiled roofs and a new kind of light signalled the Mediterranean and Languedoc-Roussillon. I turned the music up as we descended – The Mavericks' 'Dance the Night Away'.

The words, the southern light, and the warm air cartwheeling through the open windows seduced us into singing along together. A celebration of sorts. We each of us knew that what we'd left behind could no longer reach us, and what was to come might be better, if only because it was unknown.

It is night when we arrive at Phil's farmhouse.

Nothing has changed since he moved in twenty years before. A Belling oven, peeling wallpaper dating back to the thirties, concrete floors painted to imitate tiles, bare wires protruding from the walls. The window of the French doors is still broken, just as I remembered, held together with peeling yellowed Sellotape, the result of an incident involving his ex and a shotgun she was brandishing that fortunately didn't go off.

The three of us are easy together through the evening, sitting by the wood burner and chatting, eating pizza my daughter and I had picked up on the way. We drink a lot of wine, more wine than usual, to recover from the journey and the sense of dislocation. To amuse us in the small hours, I bring my laptop to the table and log in to the dating website Guardian Soulmates.

I had only signed up as a kind of house-warming present for Phil and myself. We were, after all, two single men of a certain age in danger of losing our perspective under the joint barrage of bad luck and malign fate. I thought a dating website full of women we would never be able to date might remind us life was passing us by. That was my excuse. As with so much of what I do, I'm not proud of this less-than-serious attitude, but there it is.

To be fair to myself, I had another motive for signing up. I wanted to state publicly that I was done with the past, free of all that, and thinking now only of the future. I had been divorced for a few years, but my ex and I still spoke almost daily, for reasons hard to fathom though easy to rationalize when you have children in common. And then there was Marie. We'd had a home together, and although that had come to an end a year before, I was still hurting from the loss, and I knew Marie was too. We had loved each other very much. Taken together, I felt I'd been in two car wrecks, one after the other, and leaving the carnage and the debris behind was now something I could do if I wanted to. I was, after all, single, and I had been single for the longest period in my entire adult life – admittedly only a year – so there was no reason I shouldn't take my seat on the love train that was Soulmates.

I'd never imagined I would do such a thing, because for a man of my generation, there is something of a stigma attached to online dating. I mean, isn't there? Searching for cars, clothes and books online feels fine. But can you really do the same with a potential lover? Some part of me felt that internet dating was for those whose mistake was in hoping for too much, indeed expecting too much, from love and life.

When I'd signed up in England, I'd taken a quick look at the profiles, just out of curiosity. I was frankly overwhelmed by the sensitive self-portraits stating life's disappointments and hurts, whole paragraphs of confessional prose charting the slow process of healing through time, hinting at permanent scars and new-found strength of character through suffering. There were touchingly tentative suggestions for an ideal mate from some of the women, as if asking for anything more than a sense of humour and a whiff of fidelity might be tempting the gods. I was clearly not the only one with low expectations, and I was genuinely moved, but also paralysed.

But things change, wine works, and so, moving the remains of the pizza to one side, I suggest the three of us could look at some profiles. No clicks will be involved, no likes, no messages of encouragement: an innocent diversion without real-world implications.

My daughter is immediately up for it. And as we kick off, her opinions on the women whose profiles we look at quickly become both outspoken and occasionally uncharitable.

'Hold on, "satisfy my spiritual needs"? What does she want, a priest? Moving on.'

Phil is frankly horrified, certainly by the indulgence of paying for the privilege, but it's more than that. His is not the cynic's reaction, but the romantic's. I can see from his frown and his reluctance to engage that he thinks I've somehow desecrated the very notion of love, and it takes him some time to warm to the idea. A minute, maybe two. Then he pulls his chair closer to get a better view. The more my daughter and I pass swift critiques, the more he is tempted to hold us up with a benevolent reservation about the dismissal we've issued. His charity doesn't last, and six or seven candidates later, his own verdicts are just as hasty.

That said, there are several women we've seen who are utterly charming in their self-deprecating words, apparently grounded and very alluring. 'Out of my league' might be another way to put it. The 'like' button is only a click away, and the temptation hovers in my mind to give what is, after all, merely an innocent compliment with no expectations.

No. In a week, my daughter – one of my two real-life soulmates, along with her sister – will be returning to the UK. I don't know when I will see her again and I know I will be bereft. I want her to think of her dad, and indeed her dad's best friend, as okay. We're still in the game, still hoping for the best, just like the women whose profiles we're scrolling through. Like them, we're survivors. That's all.

And then it happens.

Her name is GreenGenie, or rather her username is GreenGenie, written like that, one word and two capitals. She's pretty, but then so are many other women on the site. She says she's environmentally aware, works in the sector, and is extremely independent, but I skim the words of her profile because already I feel that I recognize this woman, even though I am certain I have never met her before in my life. And all because of one photograph.

It's a grey day. She sits on a wooden breakwater on a beach somewhere, with one leg extended. She's looking down, long brown hair worn loose, swept from right to left, tousled by the wind. Her jeans are ripped at one knee only; not a fashion statement, not a tear at each knee, but a careless thing, a fact. A thin pinkish-purple cardigan over a white T-shirt, a long back, and her pose – one hand between her legs, the other behind her – shows her straight shoulders to perfection. She has a walker's small green rucksack, just visible. And she wears loafers for shoes, relaxed, impractical, insouciant. I notice her fingers are long and slender. If she doesn't play the piano, she paints. For sure. And she's smiling, laughing really, her eyes averted from the camera as if shy at the moment of having her photo taken. By whom, I wonder. I study her face. There is something reserved in her expression, thoughtful, maybe even sad, an untouchable core, and yet I can tell she's strong, down to earth and completely of this world.

She is also, in short, the one.

'That's her,' I say, without for a moment doubting my absolute instinct that this stranger is everything I've ever desired or admired in a woman. When I look at my daughter and my oldest friend, I can see they think I mean Genie is fanciable, or my type, or just plain beautiful. And she is. But what I'm trying to say is so much more than that.

Because I know her intimately even though we've never met. Perhaps, I think, I've been waiting all my life just for her. Perhaps everything that has led me to this place and this time, all the confusions, the mistakes and crimes, every success, every failure, every happy love affair, every miserable break-up, every tiny, insignificant decision I've ever taken – to get on a bus, to turn left instead of right, to wear shorts all year round – the accumulation of the whole kit and caboodle has been an elaborate journey designed to bring me to this woman and to bring her to me.

'She's the one, don't you see?' I say plaintively. I look to my daughter for support.

'She's pretty,' she says.

Not even my own daughter understands, and as for Phil, sceptical doesn't begin to cover it.

It's late. The wine has flowed and my two companions are on the same side in this debate. They look at me indulgently, like I've got carried away or I'm drunk. But I haven't got carried away, and while I may be drunk, I've never been so sure of anything in my life. I'm in the grip of an epiphany, and the only way to prove it, the only thing I can do under the circumstances – short of jumping into the car and driving back to England – is to click 'like'.

Phil looks stern. 'You said you wouldn't do that.'

'I know.'

And it's liberating. All my reservations about myself evaporate in that instant. I haven't forgotten who or what

I am; it's just no longer relevant. Of course I'm unworthy, just as all lovers feel themselves to be unworthy in the presence of the loved one. But this is love at first sight, the real thing ... this is how it's supposed to be, how it's meant to be. Isn't it?

The next day, there's a message in my inbox from the Guardian Soulmates support team. The subject line reads: *Someone at Soulmates likes you back.*

It can't be. I open the mail and click on the link. My heart beats faster. I allow myself to hope. I'm nervous and sweaty and my hand shakes as I go through to the site. It's from her. It's Genie.

Barely able to focus, I read this:

I'd like to reply but I don't have a subscription right now. I'll be in touch when I do ...

Underneath, a message from the support team reads: *Please be aware that GreenGenie isn't a subscriber so has only been able to send you a one-line response selected from a list.*

I'm sitting at my father's desk in his study, and I'm looking at profiles on a dating website. This one is called Plenty of Fish. And it's free to use. Which is a bonus, as it makes my investment in the whole process low, entirely in keeping with my expectations.

Because I'm acutely aware that I am probably mad

to consider internet dating again, especially with Mum due home in only a few weeks. I should give it up, of course I should, just as I should never have gone for the Guardian Soulmates site, especially as I had just moved to France and couldn't date. But I did find Genie, even if she no longer had a subscription and could only write a one-line response, she did try to send me a message, and that alone gives me hope. Had the fates been kinder, had I had any way of contacting her, I would have done so, because the feelings I had then were real to me, and linger still.

I had no choice. I had to let Genie go. But it's hard to accept that from here on in, it could just be me, or me and Mum, until … I'm not sure I want to pursue that thought. The prospect makes it hard to let go of this possible lifeline altogether, however tenuous, however ridiculous it may seem to others, and even to me, for a couple of very good reasons.

First, my mother has a release date from the care home of April 27th. That's four and a bit weeks away. I may know very little about caring for someone in her condition, but I am in no doubt that the idea of dating at a time like this is, frankly, absurd.

Second, from what I can tell, there seem to be two distinct species of fish inhabiting the local waters, neither of which would regard me as interesting bait. I can't find one who states openly that what is missing in her life is a man in his mid fifties, losing his hair, unemployed, a soon-to-be carer for his mother, unable to take a night off, let alone go on a Caribbean holiday, with a serious shortage of what my father referred to as 'material goods', property being far and away the most significant.

Some of the women I'm reading about run their own businesses and want a man with similar status. Some of the women go to the gym. A lot. They like men with muscles, tattoos and intimate body piercings. They list the television soap operas they prefer and proudly state their love of 'footie'. Partying and clubbing are high priorities. And while they might be more sympathetic to my lack of status, I'm pretty sure the absence of a decent spread of tats and a woeful lack of interest in football might just be deal-breakers. As for clubbing … that train has left the station.

I mean no offence, either to the women of this area or indeed to the dating site, but I have to be realistic.

This is a *dating* website. You're expected to go out to dinner, clubs, pubs, football matches, theatres, cinemas – the list goes on. Only then do you earn the cosy nights in. And would those be here, with my mother sleeping down the hallway? With carers coming and going? Think of the logistics. Actually, don't, it doesn't bear thinking about.

Do you know this phrase? *Lasciate ogne speranza, voi ch'intrate*. The Italian is usually translated as the more familiar 'Abandon all hope, ye who enter here.' The quote comes from Dante's *Inferno*, one of the medieval world's great long poems, alongside Boccaccio's *Decameron* and our own *Canterbury Tales* by Geoffrey Chaucer. Dante reads the inscription as he passes through the gate of hell, guided by the shade of the Roman poet Virgil. All around them they hear the terrible cries of 'the Uncommitted ... those who lived without infamy and without praise'.

I don't know that looking after my mother will fall into the category of a descent to the underworld, but I am certain that, likely as not, I will court both infamy and praise in taking on the task of carer. And doing it alone is pretty scary.

Dante has Virgil and then later Beatrice to guide him; Beatrice, the incarnation of beatific love and a figure most scholars now agree was based on a real woman by the name of Bice di Folco Portinari. Dante met her only twice in his life – once when they were both children, and once a decade later when Beatrice, or Bice, happened to walk past him in the street, accompanied by two older women, and acknowledged him with the merest wave. This simple act caused the nineteen-year-old Dante to swoon with love, a love that would dominate his thinking and his writings for the rest of his life. Although the original Beatrice died when she was just twenty-four years old, Dante gave her an afterlife in both his *Divina Commedia* and *La Vita Nuova*, a book entirely dedicated to expressing his love for her in both poetry and prose. Writing about her was as close as he got to being with his great love, though he lived to be fifty-six, precisely the age I am now. That's love for you. Old-style courtly love. Have things really changed so much between thirteenth-century Florence and Plenty of Fish?

Una Vita Nuova – a new life – is beginning right here, right now, deep in the burbs, whether I like it or not. I will try to find a travelling companion for the trip ahead. And even if the odds look pretty hopeless, that is not the deal I made with myself. There is no point in making myself either a martyr or a monk. No point in sacrificing one life to preserve another. That would be a zero-sum game my mother would never approve of and I could never sustain.

So, maybe this is not the time to give up. Maybe this is precisely the time to go boldly into the future, my way lit by hope.

There's only one way to find out. And so, despite the strong scent of déjà vu, despite Genie, despite my circumstances, I fill in the Plenty of Fish profile and choose some photographs of myself in exotic holiday locations. I do this as a way of giving myself a foreign, slightly unclassifiable air. And I'm open about Mum.

I say I was living in France and have come back to take care of my ailing parent following my father's death; a little too much information, but true.

And then I wait.

VII

It's homecoming day.

I can't believe it. But there it is on the classic motor-cycles calendar bought from the pound shop and pinned to the side of the cooker.

The twenty-seventh of April. A date that seemed so far away for so long, it had simply become another illegible scrawl among the appointments and visits from social services, occupational therapists and all manner of health professionals. Now, it is here. This afternoon, at two o'clock, just after lunchtime at the care home, I will bring my mother back to the bungalow she once shared with my father. She has not been here for two years now, ever since the day I took her to the home, a place that was for her both purgatory and exile.

I've booked a specially adapted black cab to transport her. I will drive separately in the little red Honda with her things; that way we can save moving her out of the wheelchair and into a car seat. And I will want the taxi driver to help when we get to the bungalow, because even with Mum in her wheelchair, I don't want to take the risk of getting her out of the car and into the house on my own, not on our first day together.

You'd think, wouldn't you, that after six weeks to prepare, I'd be ready to receive my charge. And I am, I guess. I've put what we might need in place, but with so little experience to go on, I can't be sure of exactly what we do need. The hospital bed, metal-framed and wheezing gently as the electric motor pumps air through the mattress, is in the dining room as Dot suggested. It sits beneath a cabinet full of spare plates. The dismantled dining table now languishes forlornly in the garage, the leaves and legs bundled together with tape on the concrete floor like a hostage victim. My father would turn in his grave to see all this.

I've ordered incontinence pads online in lieu of a completed incontinence form that will give us access to free supplies, as I must wait until Mum is here to monitor fluids in and fluids out over the course of a week. There are blue super-absorbent ones for the night, and smaller yellow ones for the day. I may have over-ordered on the pads, but I'm told we could be changing them three or four times a day, and a new order takes weeks to arrive. I've done the calculation on that basis and written a reminder on the motorcycle wall calendar for when the time comes. I've put some blue and some yellow pads in the bedside cabinet, strategically placed next to the hospital bed, alongside medications, creams, hairbrushes and even a lipstick. I'm rather proud of my forward thinking and I can only hope the carers award me Brownie points when they see what I've done.

Social services, so dubious about the plan at the beginning, have become much more supportive as time has gone by, reassured that we're self-funding and won't be asking for money. Wheels are in motion and I have been genuinely surprised and delighted by their positive attitude in meeting our needs without red tape and with a display of largesse that does credit to our system and offers hope for the future.

The care home, too, has become less suspicious and more cooperative. The manager confirmed the date of Mum's release in writing, and fortunately, the accounts department has accepted that she can leave before they have the outstanding monies owed to them, now almost thirty thousand pounds in total.

I have already met a couple of the carers, albeit simply to say hi. I feel lucky to have found Dot's agency after so much effort and disappointment, and I can see now how difficult I made the search by insisting I wanted to be hands-on with the care. That's just not the way things work. Either you employ carers to care, or you do it yourself. Mixing professionals with family is highly unusual.

There are two good reasons why I've stuck to my guns, and a third if you include sheer ignorance. The first and most important is the whole notion that my mother should be cared for by those who love her and who are familiar to her. She has had strangers, albeit compassionate strangers, looking after her in the care home. Here, *I* will be looking after her, a tad incompetently perhaps, but with good intentions and a personal connection. The second, rather more prosaic reason is that with probate still not sorted out, we're short of money. What there is, mostly courtesy of my sister's dwindling savings, will go further with just one professional carer visiting four times a day.

I have even earned a qualification in the course of my extensive preparations for Mum's return. After signing the contract with Dot, I did a manual handling course to protect the agency's public liability policy should anything go awry. A perfectly reasonable request. The course took an hour and a half, and now, certificate in hand, I look forward to becoming a key member of the team for the first official care visit, at six thirty this evening.

But I can't think that far ahead. And I'm pacing, again.

I have made a huge lasagne for supper, with as much love as I could muster and in sufficient quantity to feed the two of us for a week. I've bought some jars of baby food, stewed apple and so on, some yoghurt and plenty of soft fruit, because I don't really know what will work best with her dysphagia. I've got soups and buckets of ice cream for the same reason. I can't think of anything else, but if I have missed something, I can always get it tomorrow, or the next day, or the day after that. I hope.

Preparations complete, trial and tribulation behind us, the scene is set, and as Mum's support act, I only await the star of the show. I check the kitchen clock and see it's after twelve. Curtain up.

At the care home, I find the reception desk deserted, as it often is at lunchtime, when it's all hands on deck to feed and water the residents.

I hesitate before going into the day room, suitcases in each hand and another under my arm, glancing towards the manager's office to see that it's dark and deserted. Surely I should be engaged with some kind of formality before retrieving my mother. But there's no one around to advise or tell me what to do, so I leave the cases by the reception desk and go through to the orangery, the day room, to find it, too, is almost deserted. Lunch is in progress, but I'm relieved to see that Mum is in her usual chair. Somebody must know today is the day. I sit next to her, and Rosa, one of the senior carers, comes over.

'Hello. Mum is going today, isn't she?' she asks.

'Yes, I'm just going to pack up the room.'

'Do you want us to help you? I can get someone.'

'I can probably manage, thank you.'

'You know where to go?'

'Yes, room thirty-six.'

I push open the door and realize how seldom I have been in Mum's bedroom before today. I simply haven't had cause. All the residents, except those who are bed-bound, are woken early and brought downstairs for the day. But I have also avoided it because I have not wanted to see where she has spent so many nights alone. I try to put those thoughts out of my mind.

I've done so little to make this room hers over the time she has been here. There is the radio by her bed, which I had hoped would keep her company, but which I notice is unplugged, with the aerial folded away. On the broad windowsill are the photographs in frames I brought with me when she first came here. There is one of my daughters, arm in arm; one of me in France; another of my sister taken in Vancouver, and there's one of the whole family, including my father and my ex-wife. That was taken on a day out to Windsor Great Park, many years ago now, when the children were small and I was still married. We all look surprisingly happy.

I lay the cases open on the bed and open the pine wardrobe, removing dresses and cardigans and shirts from their hangers and folding them without much care, knowing I'll wash everything when we're home. I notice her initials and her room number on every single item, and I remember the smell of the black permanent marker I used to write them. It occurs to me I may skip the washing altogether when I get back to the bungalow, and just throw the whole damn lot away. I pack away the radio and the slippers and some large cotton knickers, all in white and all the same. I check the en-suite bathroom, just as you do when leaving a hotel room. It's cold, though clean and functional. I can imagine Mum in her shower chair and the uniformed carers either side of her. Did she know where she was? Did she know why?

I've left the photographs on the windowsill until last, and I am about to pack them away when I see the white orchid in a pot behind them. I bought a white orchid with us on the first day, so this must surely be the same one. It's still in its small transparent pot, and is in full flower and remarkably healthy, especially considering I had bought it at a garage when I stopped for fuel on the way to my parents' house earlier that day. I make up my mind to leave it where it is. Perhaps it will be a comfort for the next occupant of the room.

Just at that moment, a carer I have not seen before pops her head around the open door. She tells me Rosa sent her to make sure I was okay. I tell her I'm fine to finish up and ask her if she would like to have the orchid. 'No!' she says. 'You must take, for good luck. Always flower, always that one, never stop.'

When she goes, I close the cases and ferry them to the car. I come back especially for the magical orchid and put it carefully on the front passenger seat. I hope the move won't disturb the karma. I hope I can keep the plant healthy at the bungalow. I want to believe in its power.

I bring back a large cardboard box with a variety of goodies inside and put it on the bench in the still-deserted reception. There are two dozen twenty-five-centilitre bottles of wine and some cute boxes of chocolates, together with a range of biscuits and sweets, sufficient to be shared among the many carers, with, I hope, something for everyone. I want this little gesture of thanks to go to the staff, not the managers. I leave the box in reception with a note for Magda, the receptionist.

It's now a quarter to two. Back in the day room, I find Mum is dozing in the second-hand wheelchair I bought from eBay for fifteen pounds. Most of the residents are back in their chairs after lunch, but Mum's armchair is empty now, and I wonder who will sit there in the future. As we wait for the taxi to arrive, there's still no sign of a manager. I'm miffed. I want some ceremony, some recognition that we're going and not coming back, some sense that this is a big thing.

We sit in silence as a large screen is wheeled into place in preparation for an afternoon bingo session. I give Ruby a little wave when she looks in our direction. I scan the horizon for Theresa, but can't find her, and then I see Clayt at the other end of the room, leading her towards the bathroom. I wish her a silent goodbye to the soundtrack of a staccato electronic voice coming from the bingo machine: 'All the sevens, seventy-seven; three and six, thirty-six.' And all at once I realize that while my mother may not miss this place, I will.

We've made it from the care home to the bungalow without a hitch and are sitting side by side in the garden, looking out on the dry ornamental fountain with its gravel and its stone figures: a cherub and a tortoise, and what appears to be a model of the children's book character Noddy in his car. Mum is wrapped up against the chill air; though the sun is making an appearance from time to time, there isn't much heat in it yet, and the grass is still wet from the morning rain. She blinks when the wind grows stronger, and squints when we turn to face the sun. I get the sense that she is more awed by being outside in the weather than by the sudden shift in location – the whole experience is new and perhaps even overwhelming for her to take in. We've been teleported from one world to another quicker than either of us can comprehend, and it's only half past two. I should be calm and content. Instead, I am high as a kite, and I just can't seem to stop talking.

'I want to show you all the things I've done. I've planted some pots for you with daffodils, and this one has irises – you like irises, don't you? And I've got the fountain going, too, though you have to fill it with the hose. Anyway, plenty of time for all that; you're home now and I'm going to take care of you, with some help, of course.'

Mum says nothing. She does not even acknowledge me. Sudden teleportation must be a huge shock to the system, which is why I thought I might ease us into our new life by sitting here in the garden a while. Does she remember any of this? Is she expecting to see my father come around the corner at any moment? Does she know who I am? There is so much I want to ask her and show her, and there's still almost four hours to go until the first care call this evening. I have no idea what to do next, but I know I've got to fill those hours in a meaningful way, preferably without talking the poor woman to death.

I stand and turn the wheelchair to face the open conservatory doors with the plastic ramps designed to make taking her inside a doddle. 'What's that scraping sound?' I say, as I prepare my run-up to the ramp. 'That's your foot, what's that doing trailing on the ground? It's going to take me a while to get used to all this, isn't it?'

'Mmm …' she mumbles, quite audibly and with unmistakable irritation.

In the dining room, I point out the pictures of my daughters hung in place of my father's laughing Cavaliers, and her bed, the hospital bed, facing the window. There's a tricky moment as I negotiate the door frame on our way into the hall, and I tell her I've slaved to clean the kitchen, ready for us to cook together. She seems nonplussed. I want to ask her how it feels to be home. But I'm afraid to ask. It's way too soon, and in any case, I'm not at all convinced she really knows she *is* home. Nor am I sure that my new personality, part desperate estate agent, part camp bellhop, is helping the orientation process.

'I'll bring tea. And some cake.'

I'm standing, or rather leaning, legs braced, my face flushed and my breathing fast, partly with the effort of pulling her forward in the wheelchair, the better to breathe, but also through sheer panic. Mum, whose own skin colour is changing before my eyes from red to purple, is pouring forth streams of clear sputum, and there's nothing I can do except mop it up with tissues as I struggle to hold her in position.

My home-made lasagne, chopped up into tiny squares on the plate, has scarcely been touched. We managed maybe two mouthfuls before she started to cough, gobbets of meat and pasta blasting from her mouth. The technical term is dysphagia. The reality is your loved one apparently choking to death in front of you, and what's worse, because of you; because I was arrogant enough to believe that so-called 'good food' could circumvent biology with wishful thinking. And all at once, I'm scared and angry with myself, and alone.

What the brain does in such situations – my brain, anyway – is both logical and absurd. Its retrieval mechanism begins frantically searching for previous experiences, learned strategies, and even hearsay. Mine is on a fruitless mission to recall the name of a procedure that might be the work of a Heindrick or a Hemlick, and might save my mother's life. Only it's not just the name that escapes me, it's the procedure itself, something I realize now really ought to have been part of my preparation for the role of carer. A parallel search is going on in the archives of my experience with my daughters as children. But neither a stout clap on the back nor putting Mum over my shoulder are feasible. So I continue to hold her forward in the wheelchair, to mop up the spittle with tissues and to offer her the glass of lemonade that I just now almost knocked to the floor. Biology and my own stupidity brought me to this place, and all I can do is make sure I do nothing more stupid and hope that biology comes to our rescue.

It does, and little by little she recovers sufficiently for me to run to the kitchen for fresh tissues and to start thinking on my feet by grabbing a spoon and a tub of ice cream from the freezer. Perhaps the ice cream will coat her airway and ease whatever is stuck there. I feed her small spoonfuls, watching carefully for any ill effects. I wipe away the snot coming from her nose, and she opens her eyes in anticipation of the next mouthful, just as I recall with my daughters, when foods with lashings of sugar could always be relied upon to bring a greater focus to bear in the eating process.

Thank God, the ice cream seems to be working and Mum's skin colour is returning to normal. All my attention is on what I'm doing, to the point that I notice I'm opening my own mouth as I will my mother to accept the next spoonful, so when the doorbell rings, the double chime catches me completely by surprise. I look up to see two figures in blue uniforms waiting outside.

I thought I had been saved by the bell. But we were not quite done with trauma.

The carers, Tracey and Gina, introduced themselves, breezing in with the kind of confidence that made me relax immediately. 'Leave it to us from here,' they said. I pointed out the pads in the bedside cabinet, the wipes and the nappy sacks, and asked if they wanted to see the bathroom just across the hall.

'I could show you,' I said.

'You're all right, can't get lost, can we? We'll be fine.'

I offered tea or coffee and they accepted.

But even as the kettle boiled, I could hear the debate going on around Mum. They were talking about how the sling attached, which way up it went and how it clipped onto the metal hoist. I began to worry, but told myself they must know what they were doing.

I was adding two sugars to Gina's tea when Tracey put her head round the door and, without embarrassment, asked me if I had any plasters.

I remember her words precisely. 'Mum's caught her knee on the hoist,' she said.

It was only when I was on my hands and knees below the bathroom sink, scrabbling for plasters, that I began to feel a simmering annoyance, bordering on indignation. *Mum* caught her knee? How did that work, exactly?

I unearthed plasters and Savlon and went through to the dining room to find my mother hanging precariously from the machine with the sling loose around her middle and her knees buckling under the strain of holding herself there. I could see straightaway that the sling was upside down, so I held Mum's weight, and together, after more pushing and shoving, we made it to the bed. It was a relief when they left.

✱

The graze is just below the knee, on the side of her leg. The wound is not especially big or deep, but I found it hard to watch Tracey patting a little flap of skin, transparent like rice paper, back into place before applying the plaster. I suppose I should have said something, but I didn't say very much at all, and perhaps that spoke volumes. I have to believe accidents happen and that everyone is nervous, working in a new situation with unfamiliar equipment.

Seeing my mum's old body, so fragile and delicate, tied to a metal machine with its unforgiving hardness and sharp edges, and the uniformed carers pulling and pushing her to position her on the bed, was difficult to witness. I hate that the institutional, the mechanical – all that I didn't want for her – is here, part of her first day in my care. It is true that she didn't seem to feel much pain or discomfort from the graze, and the plaster is doing its job. It's true that she had cuts and bruises in my father's care, and in the home too, and her skin is so thin and her flesh so delicate that one almost has to accept accidents are inevitable.

But the sum total of this first day has conspired to undermine my sense that this stupid plan of mine could ever succeed. I know it's only day one. But there is day two and three and four to go. And what about the night to come? I made sure the carers laid Mum on her side with pillows to support her back and her knees, but if the coughing starts again, will I hear her? I'll leave my bedroom door open and leave hers open too, I think. But it's a reality check. What have I been thinking? Did I really believe that this caring business would all be about home-made food, shared memories and happy days in the garden together?

Focus on the here and now. Sleep. The only way is up, right? Isn't that what the song says?

VIII

Three weeks into my new life as a carer, and the hardest part of the job is that every day is the same. Assuming things are going well, that is. There are no weekends of leisure, no time off for good behaviour and no respite for Mum or for me. Although the daffodils have already gone over and the birch trees behind the house are beginning to leaf, I feel like I am living in an eternal twilight. The carers punctuate our day with their comings and goings – and I'm glad to say there have been no more accidents – but the hours are long and the routine unchanging.

I'm tired, bleary tired, like I'm jet-lagged, or hung-over. I get up around six fifteen. Mum is invariably still asleep, and if I have stayed up late or drunk too much wine, or both, I'm not quite at peak efficiency, so I shower, put the radio on and make coffee, and though I shouldn't, I have a cigarette too.

Around seven, I try to give her a light breakfast before the carer arrives. I have learned to make sure she sleeps on her side at night to avoid phlegm building up in the back of her throat, causing her to cough or choke. To sit her up in the mornings on my own, I have to tuck a slippery nylon slide sheet under her torso by flipping her this way and that, then tug on the sheet to turn her from her side to her back. This is the correct method for safe moving and handling. I know, because I was taught it on the manual handling course, though now I'm on the front line, I find I can tug on the bed sheet to turn her without the disruption of rocking her from side to side to put the slide sheet in place. Even though I am relatively new to caring, I am already learning a valuable lesson.

The moment she is on her back, the coughing begins. So it is important to raise the head of the bed as quickly as possible, using the electric control unit that hangs from the rail. I also have the option of elevating the bed so I can offer her a glass of cold juice or a coffee and whatever we've decided on for breakfast without breaking my back or having to pull up a chair. I prepare drinks and food before waking her, so that as soon as she is in position and awake enough to understand where she is and what's going on, I am ready to feed and water her.

Sometimes she sleeps so deeply, unmoving all night and often unresponsive to my morning entreaties, that it's impossible, or just too cruel, to wake her before the care visit. So I'll delay things and give her some juice as the carer prepares the hoist. Then we'll remove her soaking-wet pad, take off her nightdress or T-shirt and lift her forward from the bed by her arms to slip the sling behind her. Velcro strap done up, I will wrap my arms around her from behind as the carer swings her legs to the side of the bed. We'll hold her there, supporting her back, while we move the hoist into position and attach the sling ends to the two outstretched metal arms that will lift her weight.

Once she is raised and secure, we'll shift her to the shower chair. The shower chair has a commode function – in other words, a hole in the seat and a bucket beneath – so she can use it as a toilet at any point.

Mum is doubly incontinent, and I worried about that before bringing her home. Her dignity and privacy concerned me, naturally, but also my own feelings about such forced intimacy between mother and son. When my daughters were babies and young children, I did it all. I changed nappies and cleared up vomit without a great deal of relish, though neither did I squirm at the sights and smells accompanying their early years. You get used to it. I wasn't sure it could be the same with Mum, but that was my hope.

It was her feelings that worried me most. Even with the dementia, she could be fabulously, surprisingly lucid from time to time. How would she feel if she became fully aware that it was her son who was wiping, washing and changing her?

Fortunately, preserving Mum's dignity and self-respect was never going to be my concern alone. Care agencies and all authorities with an interest in our situation may have been careful to voice their reservations tactfully, but right from the start, I had the strong sense that a son performing intimate personal care for his mother was considered, de facto, a dubious proposition, regardless of how well or badly I did it, or how sensitive I was to the issues. I wonder if a daughter would merit the same response – a daughter taking care of her father, for instance.

The carers are more than aware of Mum's dignity in this respect. Most shower her alone while I make coffee. Sometimes I help, but the intimate washing always falls to them, and I can make myself useful in holding the shower head, wrapping Mum in towels, or wheeling her back to the bed.

Where I really come into my own is when we're towelling her dry. That's when I take my chance to rub her back, talking to her all the while and telling her how she used to do this for me when I was a child. The faster I rub, the more she loves it, and she often giggles with delight until my arms tire and I tell her that's all for now. There's something special about having that intense personal connection as part of the care, alongside the professionals, and the arrangement works like a dream, most days. Only Claire prefers that I don't sing as I'm doing it.

Linen is changed completely once or twice a week, and the absorbent incontinence sheet every day. There's often a bit of leakage. Then, with toileting and showering complete and Mum wrapped in towels, we'll hoist her back into bed to be changed into day clothes, rolling her from side to side to pull on trousers and tops. When she's ready, we hoist her into the wheelchair and take her through to the living room to begin the day in earnest.

The lunchtime call is set at twelve noon, the afternoon one at four and the evening visit at seven, though the timings are proving to be approximate. If Mum needs changing during the day, we do the whole hoisting thing again, wheelchair to bed and bed to wheelchair. With the gaps between calls only a few hours, and with a range of chores to be done – feeding three times a day and administering medications four times, not to mention snacks or tea and cake – there's not a lot of leeway for failing to meet the schedule. I'm determined to get on top of this, and I will, but for now I'm content to make it to the day's end without major mishap and with some sense that I'm doing okay.

Most often, it's Lisa and me, morning and evening. There are more agency staff who cover the two daytime calls. Sometimes it's Melissa, who is in her fifties and originally from Slovenia; Zlatica from Slovakia; Kelly, a Londoner; or Debra from Transylvania. But it's mostly Lisa. I think she's taken to us in some way. Lisa works a lot, up to seven days a week some weeks, and six days most of the time. That means she can be with us twice a day, morning and evening, all week, and if there is a gap in her schedule, she'll often stop for a coffee too. Lisa is a whole new kind of strong woman, at least in my experience. She is scared of nobody and you wouldn't want to mess with her, yet there's a tender, even vulnerable side to her. She is fiercely protective of those she loves, and she has apparently brought Mum and me into the fold. When it comes to getting what we need – equipment, resources, a visit from the district nurses – Lisa goes in to bat for us. She has a way of asking for things that brooks little resistance from the powers that be.

I try to put routines in place, for me as much as for Mum. Sometimes they work, sometimes they don't. The expectation that such-and-such *should* happen round about now will often throw you completely when it doesn't. You make a meal, bring it in to her and she's fast asleep in the wheelchair, drooling. You stand there with the plate of food in one hand, a drink in the other, at a loss for a moment, before accepting defeat. You take the food back to the kitchen, return to her and wipe away the drool. You think about putting her back to bed, but the thought of the hoist and operating it alone is discouraging. Propping her up in the wheelchair is the only thing left to you, but how? Most often I get a chair from the conservatory, and a couple of pillows, and try to build a support on one side sufficient to prevent her head from sinking to her chest.

She's quiet, so for now, I can leave her. I check she's breathing regularly and go back to the kitchen. If I haven't had my own lunch or breakfast, which is normal, as I always like to sort her out first, I can try to eat what's on her plate. Assuming it's at all appetizing and not a rapidly cooling mush, chopped and mixed the better for her to swallow. If I don't want whatever it is, our resident fox will enjoy yet another feast later this evening.

But it's not the chores that are tiring. Doing something is not the hard part, because then you feel useful and engaged. It is the hanging around, the waiting. I am on yellow alert all day long – watchful, even nervous, but with no action I can take to bring the alert level down – and sometimes at night too, though I am blessed to have a mother who generally sleeps well and has a good appetite. In the evenings, I don't watch television much. I'm just too tired, and the outside world seems too remote to comprehend.

If I sound a little hunted, I don't mean to complain, only to explain. It's not all bad. Not at all. There's the satisfaction of a job well done. There's a role, clearly defined, obviously useful and apparently selfless. Mum is now the centre of things. The bungalow has effectively become the smallest care home in the area, with one resident and one live-in carer. The only modification it needs to be perfect as a care home is a disabled-access 'wet' bathroom. I'm on to that right now, getting quotes and pushing hard to ensure the work is done before the celebration of life and Mum's homecoming party, now only two weeks away.

But with the day done and Mum sleeping peacefully, there's time for me to reflect. Why I ever thought it possible I could internet-date once she was home is difficult to imagine now, but I guess I hoped that if I could kick things off before she arrived, there might just be a chance I could find someone who might take all this in their stride. That was overambitious given that I only had a few weeks to scroll through profiles, make contact and respond to 'likes' of my own, but I did manage to squeeze in three dates, and I'm not sorry I made the effort, even if things didn't work out quite as I had hoped.

The first date turned out to be a little scary. But then I spook easily, especially when confronted by heartfelt castration fantasies, clearly a strong instinct in Grace, whose husband had only very recently run off with his personal assistant. Certainly there was venom in her voice and a flush to her cheeks as she described the revenge she had in mind. The swiping movement she made with her right hand added conviction and a vivid illustration of exactly how she might go about it.

We met in a pub called the Windmill. They serve thrice-cooked chips in little tin buckets, and sea bass fillets with Thai seasoning. I was glad we were there only for a drink and would not require knives or forks.

I didn't call her again, but I did write an email to say thank you, explaining that I had thought better of my situation and realized that my new incarnation as a carer would preclude relationships of any meaningful kind. True, but convenient too.

Date number two, Jennifer, proved to be a very different affair, and one that still delights me even today, many moons after the one short evening we spent together. In her profile, she described herself as athletic and tall, and her profile pictures certainly gave that impression.

When I parked on the edge of the large village green we'd agreed as a rendezvous, I saw a woman who fitted Jennifer's profile waiting in her car. There was a moment's embarrassment as we established by looks and gestures that I was almost certainly him and she was definitely her, but in truth I had little reason to doubt it. When she got out of the car and we walked towards each other, I was absolutely certain that the five-foot-eleven athlete with the air of an aristocrat and the grace of a woman who knew her own value was not just my date for the evening, but also laughably, absurdly *trop belle pour moi*, as the French so delicately put it.

Once we'd sat down opposite one another and ordered a drink, I couldn't hide my sense that I was unlikely to be her dream man – ten years older, desperately unfit and balding to boot. I was laughing, and though she too saw the funny side, she demurred politely and even went so far as to find some other reasons why it was unlikely we could make a relationship work. Both her children were British Olympic team athletes and her time was largely dedicated to their needs – and it was she who drew the comparison with my situation, which was fabulously gallant of her. We giggled a lot that night. She was interested in and concerned about my becoming a carer, and genuinely impressed. That was quite something for me to hear. In return, I asked enthusiastic questions about her life as an athlete. We said goodbye outside the pub with a chaste kiss and a metaphoric bow to the fates, and though we've spoken on the phone since, I don't expect we'll meet again.

Date three was Ellie. In fact, she turned out to be date three *and* date four, which may seem promising in terms of love, but actually wasn't. Not that my third date was in any way unpleasant. Ellie chose a pub with a fine garden area and a decent menu, situated close to her home – for the sake of convenience, she said, entirely unabashed.

The evening was warm enough to sit out. The air was humid, encouraging evening walkers, some of whom were heading towards the same pub.

I arrived early and settled myself at an empty table, and when I saw Ellie walking through the garden, I knew instantly it was her. There was something quick in her stride, perfunctory in the way she scanned the assembled drinkers. Her profile opened with an aphorism she said was her motto: 'What comes easy won't last. What lasts won't come easy.' I wondered which category our evening would fall into. Our brief exchange of hellos had no suggestion of any frisson, as if Ellie might be here under sufferance. Though it was far too early to draw conclusions, I was on my guard.

I came back from the bar with a Pinot Grigio – large, because small might appear mean – to find her smoking a cigarette.

'I saw that you smoke, which was a relief,' she said. I mumbled something about bad habits as I sat down, and tried to recall details from her profile that might spark conversation. She had a morbid fear of flying, she was not necessarily 'looking for the one', and she was interested in photography, but I need not have worried. Ellie liked to talk, and she was good at the kind of conversation that was light and easy enough for two strangers to sustain. I got the distinct impression that she had vastly more experience of dating than me, especially first dates.

We ordered food and sat opposite each other at a small table that was just a little too intimate for a first date. Sometimes these things catch fire, and sometimes they don't. We were easy enough together, but any real connection eluded us. We both declined pudding, and I had the strong sense she was as happy to end the evening as I was.

As we were paying the bill at the bar, she realized she'd forgotten her purse. She was embarrassed, and there followed a good deal of conjecture as to how such a thing could have happened. I made it clear that I was more than happy to pay and we should consider the incident to be an act of God. I certainly didn't feel the forgotten purse constituted any kind of obligation between us, despite her protestations.

The next day I got an email from her saying, with admirable directness, *Well, I think you'll agree, there's no spark between us.* I did. Only there was more. She said she could not bear the thought that the purse thing might seem like a deliberate strategy to get a free meal. I assured her the thought had never crossed my mind, that she should feel herself absolved of any indebtedness, that it had been a pleasure to meet her and that perhaps one day, at some point in the future, we would meet again.

She wrote back insisting on returning the compliment and buying me lunch. With only a couple of days to go until Mum came home, I reluctantly gave in, as the only way to satisfy her honour.

The lunch was just like the supper in all respects, bar the fact that this time she'd brought her purse. She dutifully paid for us both, and when we stepped outside to say our goodbyes, she began to go through the bill in fine detail. Something was wrong. I was wondering how to make my escape when she realized she had been undercharged by twenty pounds. Her obvious joy at having bucked the system charmed me and made me laugh, which in turn made her laugh, and in that moment, all awkwardness between us evaporated.

You can't laugh at a potential lover, but we both knew we were not about to become lovers. Any and all tensions on that question had been laid to rest, clearing the way for us to become mates. Ellie lived nearby, and a girlfriend she often went cycling with had a house just around the corner from the bungalow.

'I'll give you a call when I'm passing,' she said. 'Pop in and see how you're doing, shall I?'

'Do, I'd like that.'

I have no excuse for believing a companion for my journey might have been waiting for me online, save the classic triumph of hope over experience. As a carer, or trainee carer, it's difficult, impossible really, to express the odd combination of constant visitations and complete isolation your life comprises, with every day just like every other, with your own existence reduced to that of a functionary, a bit player, an amateur among professionals, a man among women, and a novice in a hermetic world where carers, as the name implies, simply care, their lives dedicated to the service of others.

Still, I'm glad I tried. Nothing comes from nothing, and in trying, I may just have made a friend.

Perhaps that's enough.

SUMMER

IX

Now that Mum is more settled, I take my chance to explore when I know she is safe or asleep. It is impossible to care for her without going into the outside world from time to time, to shop, pick up medications from the chemist, and just to get a break; early mornings are best, but the evenings – when she is soundly sleeping – can be another opportunity. If I need more time, I ring the agency and one of the carers will sit with her for a few hours.

My early forays in Dad's red Honda revealed an unexpected aspect to my brave new world: large areas of open heath, some of it army land and given over to firing ranges, stretching to more than three thousand acres, or so I'm told. From the bungalow, on quiet days when the motorway traffic is lighter, you can clearly hear the dull booms and thumps of distant artillery, though I had to ask a neighbour to explain what it was

I was hearing. But there are also stretches of common land where people can park up and walk dogs, ride bikes and explore. Though I have no dog, I have persuaded myself I should go for the occasional walk, for my own good.

I feel conspicuous walking alone on the trails, and still find myself inclined to say bonjour as I pass other people, only adding to my sense of dislocation. Our family dog, Maisie, is old now, almost thirteen, but before the divorce she was a good excuse to go for a long walk every single day. The home I shared with my wife until the divorce is situated close to the South Downs in Sussex. There were breathtaking views to soak up as Maisie followed her nose to hunt stray pheasants lurking in the undergrowth. Our family walks were long, often three or four hours, and sometimes ended at a pub with a pint of bitter for me, lemonades for the girls and bags of crisps to share with the dog.

The elevation of the Downs meant big skies and long vistas for thirty miles or more, and so I seldom felt short of sunlight, even in winter. Since then, France has spoiled me with blue skies and sun, though the stretches of heathland here do compensate with their blue heathers and brown grasses stretching into the distance. The local woodland is mainly plantation conifers, but I have found patches of deciduous wood, where oaks and birch and beech trees abound and grass and flowers grow on the ground beneath, picnic places I may never get to use but that remind me of times past.

I should walk more often, because the fresh air clears my head and brings a kind of objectivity to my situation, allowing me to stand back from events and sometimes to indulge in ruminating on how I found myself here, treading pine needles and skirting puddles in second-hand wellington boots. Only this week, I found myself thinking a lot about the idea of home.

I haven't had a home to call my own since the divorce settlement decreed I should move out of the family house in return for half of its value. For the first few weeks, I stayed with my friend Jojo, who happened to live on the same road in the same town as my old home. Jojo lived alone in a large house and had a way of knowing when people were in trouble, and providing a refuge for a variety of waifs and strays. I thought I might lick my wounds and recover from the shock of losing so much in such a short space of time. That was a mistake – I was too raw to be so close to my old life – but a woman who lived a few doors down from Jojo had an aunt who owned a tiny former cowshed in France, converted to contain a rudimentary kitchen, bathroom and bedroom. It was now boarded up for the winter, but she said I could stay there for a peppercorn rent if I was willing to do some work around the place. If I stuck to bread and cheese and cheap wine, I might be able to preserve my share of the capital from the house and live modestly off the interest.

Although the move would mean being six hundred miles away from my daughters, I would have a place of my own for them to stay. With money in the bank, I could fly home to see them and visit my parents. The girls could come out for regular holidays, where they would find their once miserable father living cheerfully in the south of France and doing what he had always wanted to do: write a book. That was the first time I ran away to France.

Marie and I were a couple by then, but we were not yet living together. She was not happy about my going, but I explained that I needed time to make the transition from marriage to a fully committed new relationship. I promised her I would visit regularly. I said the cowshed – my soon-to-be writer's garret – would also be our romantic getaway. She granted me licence because she loved me, and I took advantage.

I packed my old Subaru to the roof and drove as far south in France as you can go without being in Spain. Judith, the aunt who owned the place, had warned me repeatedly that L'Atelier, as she called it, was basic and lacked many essentials. I reassured her that was fine by me. Secretly, I was rather delighted to be heading for my very own artist's garret. The studio was situated on the Coll de Bossells – a piece of high ground looking down on the town of Céret and up at the Pyrenees. Just five kilometres from the Spanish border, Céret was Catalan in outlook as much as French, popular early in the last century with artists like Picasso and Braque and Matisse. I broke up the twelve-hour drive through France with a short stay with Phil, who lives two hours north of the cowshed. I had talked him into coming with me to help make my new home feel like a home.

We arrived at the Coll towards the beginning of March, and parked on a patch of grass outside a small stone building, shuttered and forlorn, with glass bricks in one wall that gave it the appearance of a public toilet, or an electricity substation. I found the key in the shed where Judith had said it would be, and we ventured inside, hoping to get settled before the early spring sun sank below the horizon.

I remember the screech of the door on the bare concrete floor. The interior was musty and damp and bitterly cold, and there was an odd crunch to our first footsteps that was a little alarming. The crunch turned out to be a black carpet of dead termites thick enough to obscure the floor entirely. Phil said the remains indicated a voracious ant colony, though I wasn't clear if he meant the information as reassurance or evidence of a bigger issue. Further in, we found cracks in the walls you could put your hand into and see daylight beyond. There was no heating, and no insulation in the stone walls, and a cursory examination of the electricity supply by Phil – who, being an architect, knows about such things – revealed wiring that was potentially lethal. He declared the place uninhabitable.

I disagreed. There was a kitchen table, two chairs and a gas cooker, with a door leading to a bedroom with a creaking metal-framed bed and a vintage horsehair mattress. In the corner of the bedroom, a stained sink and a rudimentary shower behind a curtain comprised the en-suite bathroom. Wooden stairs against the kitchen wall led to a mezzanine platform and a toilet, partitioned off by a thin wall but perfectly serviceable and with a flush that worked. Things were looking up. I was determined not to give in to the termites, the ants, the cold or the holes in the walls. All that could be fixed in no time, I said confidently. It helps when you feel you have no choice. So we set to it. By the time dusk fell, the termites were mostly swept away, the place was warmer, thanks to an electric heater I'd brought from England, and we'd managed to rustle up a raclette, heated by the paraffin burner of a fondue set I'd found in a junk shop before I left. We ate well to soak up the best part of a three-litre box of wine. When it came to sleeping, neither of us fancied the horsehair mattress, so we shared the wooden floor of the mezzanine, wrapped in duvets, and only slept at all because we'd drunk so much.

Over the weeks and months that followed, I worked on the novel I had been writing for ten years or more but had never got around to finishing. It was to be based on the true story of William Morgan and the part he played in the Cuban Revolution. Morgan was an outsider and a natural-born rebel who had taken a chance in a foreign country and transformed his life. It is hard to admit now that I saw parallels between my hero's life and my own, but I have to confess, I did. I set to work, writing a thousand words a day, fixing up the cowshed in the afternoons and taking myself for a swim in the sea when I needed inspiration.

As time went by, it became clear that Marie would only be content when we set up home together, and I began to want that too. My parents were struggling to live with Mum's Parkinson's, and there were already signs that she was increasingly at risk from my father. My younger daughter was unhappy. Her mother and I had decided to move her from a state school to a fee-paying one, much against our better principles. The money in the bank was steadily going down. Little by little, without ever really meaning to quit my writer's hut and my romantic existence as an artist manqué, I was drawn back into the life I'd left behind. Eleven months in, I'd written half the book, repaired the cracks in the walls and fixed the electricity supply, but it was time to go home, whatever that might mean.

★

By comparison with the challenge of making L'Atelier habitable, turning a centrally heated suburban bungalow with sealed plastic windows and carpet throughout into something like a home of my own ought to be a doddle. The problem here is not the lack of comforts, but rather the fact that the place is all too comfortable. I feel insulated from the outdoors in a way that I was not in France. So I try to get Mum outside as much as possible, to eat outside, to take my cup of coffee for a walk around the garden, and I try to motivate myself to cut the lawn my father cherished and nurtured, or to attack the hedges that have grown wild and woolly with no gardener to keep things in order as he did. His birdfeeders are empty of nuts and seeds, though there are benefits: his constant battle to keep the squirrels at bay is not a problem I have had to face to date.

The bungalow sits on the turning circle of a cul-de-sac of other bungalows, some identical, some dissimilar in a way that makes no significant difference. There are no fences bordering the tarmacked road or separating one garden from another, but the judiciously planted leylandii hedges have grown taller than the bungalows they protect. The gardens are neat and well kept, in large part because gardening is the main occupation of the mostly elderly residents. Bins go out on a Thursday – recycling one week, general waste the next. Beyond the bungalow's back garden are mature trees: aspens, smooth and grey-barked, their silvery leaves shimmering in the wind; Scots pine in the darkest of greens, and weedy birch, losing their fight for light. An unbroken line stretching as far as I can see. I'm told the trees grow on extensive land belonging to a rich man, a sultan, they say, who owns a large house somewhere down a long drive. My father loved the backdrop of trees, because their presence meant the garden was not overlooked by neighbours. But if they are a screen, they also block the horizon and add to the sense of the bungalow as an isolated hermitage.

Other than my year at L'Atelier, I have never had the opportunity to truly make a home on my own. That may be a sad fact in a grown man, but three long-term relationships over forty years – ten years with my Italian beauty, twenty as a married man and ten with Marie – amounts to a lifetime of coupledom or dependency, whichever way you care to phrase it. Of course, this is Mum's home, but with Dad's legacy everywhere. Still, I can make changes. I have a blank canvas, and to be honest, I'm excited at the prospect.

But if I get to make decisions alone, I am not used to *being* alone. Of course Mum is here, and we keep each other company. The rhythm of the day with her is familiar now, sometimes too familiar. But if I am busy in the daylight hours, I am often at a loose end in the evenings. Perhaps that's why a kind of gloom comes over me around twilight. Maybe not gloom; it might be better to say a kind of agitation, the kind that makes me want to hear a voice other than my own. I speak to one of my two daughters almost daily. I speak to Phil maybe twice a week, and I call my sister in Canada, or she calls me, once a week. I know no one in this part of the world. Those folk I do know – my ex-wife, a couple of old friends in the same town as her – are an hour and a half away from the bungalow where I'm dialling numbers to keep loneliness at bay.

I'm used to sharing the trials and tribulations of the day with someone. Of course, people who live alone can make phone calls, write emails and make social arrangements to mitigate isolation, and I'm learning to do just that in my new situation, but for me at least, it's not the same. On the phone, the audience is remote and the contact doesn't have the same immediacy. The stories I tell or listen to are pickled or preserved in some way for later consumption. I like my stories fresh and larded with banter.

But I make the calls and take the calls anyway, though afterwards, the sense of being alone is often more acute. In this unbearably comfortable bungalow, the only presence other than me and my sleeping mum is the ghost of my father. I make a last check on her to make sure she is snoring peacefully, turn her pillow, and then go to the kitchen to open a bottle of wine I don't really want and certainly don't need. There are still some hours where the choice is between going to my father's bed to read, or flicking on the television. Neither really calls to me, and I sometimes find myself wandering from room to room, hoping to find a clue as to what to do.

I have become aware of an unexpected aspect to my life here, one I suppose I could have anticipated, but didn't. I now live in a world of women. Having gone to some lengths to meet women online, the irony is not entirely lost on me.

The carers are women. The care agency manager, Dot, and the office staff I speak to from time to time are women. The two district nurses who have come by with incontinence charts and a general health check for Mum are women. Our doctor is a woman. The carers' support representative who brought me literature on keeping myself healthy, mentally and physically, is a woman called Joan with a fine line in irony concerning the life of a carer.

Lynn, the occupational therapist, has made so many visits to oversee equipment like shower chairs and hospital beds being safely delivered that I now know her favourite biscuits. Ginger nuts, as it happens. I had a call the other day from Dana, the SALT – speech and language therapy – provider. Julie also called – Lynn had told me she would – to organize a superior kind of

wheelchair for us, one that will offer more side support
and a headrest. Then there's Sylvia, the Parkinson's
nurse. She has a thick Glaswegian accent, but is soft-
spoken and full of compassion. She will visit every six
months or so, with a first visit planned just a few weeks
from now. I am frankly astonished to have so much help
from so many women.

Some men might be overwhelmed. As it happens,
I feel quite at home basking in this level of female
support, though what this imbalance between the sexes
says about the business of caring, about men and women,
and about society as a whole would take a good deal of
space and time to debate. Certainly, my new life is quite
a change from my year in France with Phil, working
together on his building site. There, we spent our days
under the hot sun nailing things together, mixing
concrete and generally doing hard physical work. Apart
from two visits by my daughters and one trip by Marie
– a vain attempt by the two of us to patch things up
after a year of separation – women were conspicuous
by their absence. We lived as two solitary monks, or as
the majority of the French believed, a typically English
couple, odd but harmless.

If some of the women I encounter have doubts
about my ability to look after my mother, or worse still,
suspicions about my motives, I also have a certain cachet
simply because I am a man. There's good and bad in this.

My gender and my role as a carer – despite the statistics that tell otherwise – is considered not just uncommon, but borderline unnatural, making me laudable and appealing on the one hand, but also 'one to watch'.

There is a significant element of performance to my new role, which only plays to my strengths. I make sure there's a good deal of chat with the carers. Banter breaks down barriers and puts us all more at ease, or so I hope.

Claire is another of our regulars, coming either for the hour-long morning call when we shower Mum, or for the evening half-hour call when we change her into nightclothes ready for bed. Unlike Lisa, who is almost always upbeat and chatty, Claire can look like she's carrying the weight of the world. She gets up at five and generally misses breakfast to get to 'the yard', where her first care call of the day is her horse, too old to ride any longer, but too beloved to be put down. She might already have done three or four care calls before she arrives here. What cheers her up is when I offer peanut butter on toast with her morning cup of tea.

If we're all becoming more relaxed in each other's company, I still find it odd that the private space of our home has become so public. This is partly circumstantial. For instance, there is no airing cupboard in the house, and the other two bedrooms are small, with very little storage. My room, my father's old bedroom, has built-in cupboards down the length of one wall. The storage is sufficient to house all the sheets, blankets and towels, along with my mother's clothes and my own paltry supply of shirts and trousers, pants and socks, one jumper and a sweatshirt, brought over in a single suitcase from France. So there is every reason for carers to come and go as they please, retrieving a fresh incontinence sheet, finding dry towels or a fresh supply of pads, whatever it might be. My personal habits – including whether I make the bed in the morning, leave my socks on the floor, or worse still, my pants – reveal more than I might choose to share. Even the partisan Lisa, on my side in all other areas, is not above making it clear how she feels about what she sees. 'That stuff on your floor could go in the machine with Mum's sheets, but you'll have to pick it up. I ain't bloody doing it.'

The implied, and sometimes openly stated 'Men!' tagged on the end of these casual observations is never more justified than when applied to the washing pile. Lumping together darks and lights apparently constitutes a terrorist action. I have never owned or operated a dryer before, and had no idea these machines routinely ruin clothes in a way that makes you wonder why anyone would risk using them. The latest victims were a couple of linen shirts I found on a sale rack, now reduced in a way I had never bargained for.

This week there has been a man among the visitors to the bungalow, someone with little interest in my ability to operate a washing machine or a dryer. Jim is ripping out the shower cubicle and digging up the floor tiles with a view to creating our new 'wet' bathroom, so we've been without a proper shower for about four days. There are heavy-duty black bags in the garage full of rubble and the old tiles. The perspex doors and a hefty shower tray made of concrete and ceramic are lying outside in the driveway. I will get it all to the local dump, but I don't know when.

A man of few words, Jim has assured me the work will be complete in time for the celebration of life, enabling guests to pee and powder their noses without going behind the bushes in the garden.

That is a real relief.

X

The last ten days have gone by in a blur.

Jim will finish the bathroom tomorrow or the day after, he says, depending on a delivery of tiles we need. They've been on order for a week and I should get a call today. We shall see.

On the plus side, my sister arrives in two days' time for the celebration of life, and the invitations I have printed at home and sent out by post or email have garnered a healthy response, with no outright objections to the notion of a buffet-cum-barbecue in the garden. I'm surprised, and relieved. The numbers will not be embarrassing. Sis will help with getting food and drink for the day. My daughters and my ex-wife have volunteered to be catering staff. Even the weather forecast looks promising.

There should be about thirty people, including a contingent of Irish relatives made up of my father's niece and her large family, flying in especially for the event and staying at a hotel nearby. Cousins, all contemporaries of mine, will accompany Uncle Pete. Harry, an old work colleague of my father's, is coming, along with his wife, and there's Big John, who I've never met but have heard talk of, a golf club acquaintance in his nineties. Then there's Bonnie, who was at school with my mother before the Second World War. It seems hard to believe that the two of them have known each other for seventy years or more. I've also taken the chance of inviting the near neighbours, who I don't know, on the basis that there was presumably at least a nodding acquaintance with my parents.

I'm making it sound like things are busy the whole time. And it's true, there are carers in and out, phone calls and correspondence with solicitors and social services, ongoing probate matters, nor have I got around to clearing the garage of all the rubble yet. But there are quiet times too. Sudden and abrupt switches from the frenetic to nothing and no one. Times when the outside world goes quiet and seems far away, even unreal. Times when it's just Mum and me.

After a meal or a snack, assuming it's gone down well, there's often a pause when nothing needs doing and we're alone in the house or sitting side by side in the garden. Now the weather is good and we can be outside, I take every opportunity, even when wind or rain threaten. In the care home, she was never outdoors, except when we visited and asked that she be hoisted into a wheelchair so we could walk the grounds. Now that it's early summer, there are days of sunshine and wilder days with scudding clouds and where the breeze is warm enough that a blanket and a shawl will suffice for Mum's needs.

I knew the outdoors would be good for her, but I am surprised to find that she knows it too. Though she hardly speaks, I talk to her – too much, probably – about being here in the garden, pointing out what is going on around us and making sure she is not cold and is happy to be here. Only the other day, when the weather was mixed and I had put her shawl over her shoulders and head, I said, 'You look like a little Russian babushka; are you sure you don't mind being out here?'

I expected nothing in return, but she was lucid and clear in her response and caught me completely by surprise, yet again. 'I love being outside,' she said.

I should have known it from the way she soaks up the sights and sounds of this very suburban garden, as if we were sitting together in an exotic landscape. She visibly feels the breeze, screwing up her nose as if to take in scents that might come to her. The movement of a bird or the sound of a plane passing overhead will attract her attention and she will look towards the source. But it is more than just noticing. I can't quite explain the calm that comes over her, except to remind myself that we can all react to the natural world in the same way, taking comfort, breathing more deeply, experiencing a sense of exhilaration at knowing we are part of something bigger than ourselves.

I want to claim more. I like to hope that out here – having been inside a centrally heated care home for so long, and confined to her own home by my father's anxiety that she might fall or hurt herself – she feels free. I have no proof, nothing to confirm this sense of things, bar the absolute conviction of my own intuition, the smile on her face and her engagement with the world around us.

These times are the most precious of all, and I must learn to cherish them and foster them, even when there is so much else to do. It's all too easy to find chores that need seeing to, or to constantly minister to Mum as a way of reassuring myself that I'm actively caring. But I try to fight the instinct to be busy when I don't have to be, and to find time simply to be mother and son; just two people together.

The dementia means she is often unaware that it is her son next to her, or even that she's at home. We can seem like strangers to each other despite our shared history. The woman beside me in the garden, just beginning to chill as the sun dips behind the apex of the bungalow roof, is certainly very like the woman I used to visit with my children; she was quiet and subdued, and when I helped her in the kitchen and asked quietly if everything was okay with Dad, she would smile with tears in her eyes and tell me not to worry. This woman is like her, but not quite her.

It occurs to me at these times that, though my mother and I have known each other all our lives, we have spent very little time alone like this, just sitting. It takes a little getting used to, each being the centre of things for the other. The dependency ought to be familiar, even if the role of caregiver has shifted from her to me, but it's not. There is so much I would like to ask her, and so much I would like to thank her for, because I have never really acknowledged her care for me, either to myself or, more importantly, to her.

Because the woman beside me really did change my nappies and breastfeed me. It was she who put me and my sister to bed at night; she who was there to make us breakfast in the morning. I am not here to pay her back for all the years of love and worry and kindness. How could anyone hope to? But it occurs to me as I watch her, absorbed in her own world, her fingers moving nimbly to pinch and gather the blanket, intent on some purpose I cannot fathom, that in these quiet moments I can at least recognize and celebrate all she's done for me, thank her silently, and even feel a touch of awe.

I can see her eyes beginning to close right now, but

still her fingers are fidgeting, and while she's never had the tremor usually associated with Parkinson's, her hands will often quiver if she tenses up, as she's doing right now. Her face is flushing with the effort of clearing her throat, and for a moment she stops breathing altogether. Finally there's a little explosion of spit, and I wipe at her mouth with tissues.

Life for my mother is winding down and wearing out. I am witness to a quadrant of it in which atrophy is the governing principle and death the inevitable end. There's something fascinating in seeing an entirely natural process at such close quarters. She is my mum, but the process of ageing makes it apparent she is also subject to the laws and rhythms of nature, continually churning life into death, inexorable and indifferent certainly, but also universal.

Only here in the garden, early summer is playing out another tune altogether. All around us are the signs of life asserting itself, flourishing in the warm sun, growing, and somehow brighter before our eyes, more vibrant and more intense. Young blue tits come and go from the hanging feeders, cheeky and careless, quite indifferent to us as we sit side by side only a few feet away. The grass is thicker and more lush than it was even a week ago, and the peonies are coming into flower.

All of which makes me wonder where I fit in. I am, after all, subject to the same laws of nature and the same inevitable process of atrophy, even if I see myself with a future beyond the role of carer, even if I am thinking about how I can delay the inevitable, or at least take my mind off it, by looking for love.

Not that I am looking any more, though a quick trawl of the Plenty of Fish website still occasionally soaks up an hour in the evening. Truth is, I've given up. I have no skin in the game, and looking online is a lazy form of entertainment, mildly more interesting than the telly. Even if I were serious, the search would be hampered, not to say hamstrung, by my own ageing process. The pace has definitely picked up recently. Maybe stress plays a part. It can't do any good. I know I've put on weight, if only because I was doing physical work in France whereas all I do here is pad around the house with trays of food, or sit at a desk to tackle paperwork. But I'm also just older, slipping down the same slide as Mum, only a little way behind her, gripping hard to the sides in order to slow the inevitable.

I can try to accept the outward signs of age, but it is more difficult to live with the aches and pains in places I have never had cause to pay much attention to before now. Ankles, knees, even finger joints occasionally flare up, for no apparent reason and with no specific cause, other than the wear and tear of many years of uncomplaining service. I have already been to the doctor twice.

Joan, who heads the local carers' support group, told me carers tend to neglect their own health, simply because their whole focus is on another person's needs. She said I should make a conscious effort to guard and promote my own well-being, though she didn't offer a palliative for the ageing process. Mental health, too, can suffer, she said, with half of all full-time carers seeing a doctor at some point for depression or anxiety, and many ending up on long-term medication. Wine is my bastion against the need for prescription drugs. Not that I say as much to the nice woman from carers' support.

XI

I am waiting at the arrivals gate at Heathrow Airport for my sister to get in from Vancouver, just in time for the celebration of life.

The information board tells me the plane landed twenty minutes ago and baggage from the flight is in the hall. I pass the time, as we all do, casually studying the arriving passengers, marvelling at the variations in human beings created by four chemical bases and two short strands of DNA.

My sister is coming towards me, pulling the same enormous blue suitcase she took away with her only weeks ago. I marvel at her stamina and commitment to the cause in coming back so soon, in spending so much money on airline tickets, but above all in being able to extricate herself from her own life when I know things are not easy for her at the moment. She is a manager at a television station, a big one, and part of her role is to handle employee grievances, redundancies and high-level negotiations with the unions regarding company policy. She is kind and conciliatory by nature, and I think it costs her a lot to mediate conflict almost daily. The work stress is only made worse by the fact that her relationship with her partner is falling apart, despite her negotiating skills.

In the car, I give her a rundown on where we are with preparations for the big day, now only forty-eight hours away. For the sake of convenience, the superstore we visited the day after Dad's death is providing most of the food.

'I'm still not sure about a barbecue,' my sister says.

'But it's what Dad would have wanted, don't you think? He always loved a—'

'Stop it.'

I am not looking to open old wounds, and nor do I want to be accused of showing disrespect, though I have to confess, I am hoping to deflect criticism for failing to hold a traditional church service, cremation or burial. I need to consult with my sister before deciding what to do with Dad's ashes, but that can wait. Right now, what I want is to give us all reasons to be cheerful on what is likely to be a gloriously sunny afternoon, and make Mum feel like queen bee.

Sis and I have talked a lot over the weeks about the potential for Mum to be disturbed or upset by the celebration. I have made every effort to mention the plan and to get her used to the idea by talking about Dad in a casual way whenever I could over our eight weeks or so together. I can't say I have had any reassuring feedback from her, which is why it crossed my mind to put a note in with the invitations asking guests to be mindful, but the truth is, it felt almost impossible to phrase without causing alarm. Far better to rely on them to do the right thing by instinct, not that I have a clear idea of what the right thing is. We will have to see what happens on the day.

As things turned out, I need not have worried. There was every reason the day might have veered off the road to end in a car crash, but it didn't. Mum was the belle of the ball. She looked fit and fabulous, thanks to Lisa, who decided on a white linen blouse over a pretty summer dress, and who took time and trouble with creams and a hairdryer, a touch of foundation and even a little lipstick. Mum looked beautiful, and incredibly calm, as if the preparations and the prospect of the celebration excited her.

Dad was prominently represented by a corkboard propped up in the conservatory. The board featured photographs that together told a chronological, if sketchy, story of two lives joined, from their wedding day to early holidays in the sixties and a later exotic posting to Nassau in the Bahamas with the airline company he worked for. I found some newspaper clippings from an airline trade paper, and a photo of him looking like a tycoon behind a large desk. I hesitated over a signed picture of Dad with Larry Hagman, the star of the TV show *Dallas*, both of them in oversized cowboy hats, but he liked it, so who was I to stand in their way?

My ex-wife showed up early to help with catering preparations. My younger daughter had hitched a ride with her and was bravely nursing a hangover as we put drinks on a trestle table and covered another with buns and wraps and sauces. My elder daughter came by train from London and I picked her up from the station, getting back just as the first guests were arriving, to find everything calm and collected, save my sister. All afternoon she made beelines between fridges and guests, refilling and restocking to the point where they avoided eye contact with her for fear of more food or drink.

The high point of the afternoon was seeing my mother respond to the attentions of those gathering around her. If she appeared a little bewildered from time to time, there were also moments when she smiled and even responded to questions and compliments. It's quite astonishing how the social function of the brain, the desire or need to be part of a group, survives the ravages of dementia. The guests were wonderful with her, attentive without being patronizing or gushy. Each took a moment to introduce themself or remind her of who they were, to ask about her and tell an anecdote or wish her well, and there seemed to me to be a genuine warmth and respect in their approach.

After three or four hours, the guests seemed to leave as one, by instinct or through decorum, melting away to their cars and houses and leaving us to clean up. Watching my sister and my daughters and ex-wife together, preparing for the celebration, tidying up afterwards, giggling as we debriefed in the garden that evening, I realized how much I'd missed being with family, not just over the time with Mum, but also during my stay in France. It had been too long since we'd all been together like that, sharing stories and laughing.

Taking my sister to the airport again so soon after her arrival, so soon after the last time we made this same journey, feels premature to us both, and a little brutal on her. She and her partner of twenty years, a former paratrooper in the Canadian Airborne, a man who shows the scars of his service to his country in the form of PTSD, are likely to split up. As is the way with these things, she has fallen out of love with her work, too, and feels she is returning to a foreign land not her own. All she really wants is to come home, to be here with her mum and to help with her care, but instead she finds herself flying away yet again.

'Don't worry about abandoning us,' I say.

'I won't, but it's odd, all journeys are circular. Maybe I'll come back. I miss being close to my family, and I miss the humour too.'

'Would it help if I took the piss out of you for a little while?'

'No.'

The garden's deserted now, except for a lot of tables and chairs still to be put away. It was hard saying goodbye to my sister, hard to say goodbye to my daughters too. But I know they will be back. The elder says she could come down and spend a night sometime soon so we get a whole evening together, and the younger will soon finish her summer term. She has a bar job lined up, but she also has a short dissertation to write. Her social life – she is singing in a pub and getting plenty of attention from boys – is hotting up and squeezing her time for college work. In return for a little editorial help from her dad, she says she too might come and stay over.

It's hard too because now the celebration of life is done, Mum and I are back to business as usual. The routine. Claire's care call on the morning after the big day, at seven thirty as always, felt like an affront, even though it was her familiar face at the door. The next call is at midday, though I have decided I am definitely going to cut that one, as Mum seldom if ever requires a change so quickly after the first visit of the day.

There was rain overnight, and the tables and chairs have droplets of water on them. Mum is sleeping in her wheelchair in the conservatory, and the corkboard with photographs of my father is still propped on the table opposite her. I can see them both as I walk around the garden, taking a chance to get some air and think about the day. It all went well; very well, in fact. Wake and party melded together, neighbours and family may have stuck to their own groups, but all the guests were chatty and relaxed and seemed to be having a good time, as far as I could tell. I should be pleased, and proud of myself too, but I feel out of sorts and grumpy – tired, probably. So much of my focus has been about getting to the celebration that it had become an end in itself. Now, I'm not sure where the next milestone lies. Ahead, more care and the same daily routine, but I can't complain; that's the deal, and I don't think that is what's niggling at me.

Instead, it is the past I am brooding on, and one insistent memory of my father from a time when my sister and I were still young enough to share a room. Mum would say goodnight and tell us that Dad would be up soon. Tucked under our blankets with only the landing light on beyond the half-closed door, we would hear his footsteps on the stairs and wait for him to come and sit at the end of our beds. We knew what to expect, and yet every time he told us the story felt like the first time. It coloured our dreams for years. It still does to this day.

The story he told was of a fisherman, Paddy Reilly by name, and a woman waiting on a stormy Irish shore, calling through the wind and the rain to her man who is likely lost at sea. Dad would expertly conjure the scene, making the sounds of the wind and describing the rain beating down on the woman wrapped in a black shawl. He talked of her lament scattered by the gale, and her reaching out to the raging waves in the vain hope her beloved would hear her and return safely. As we snuggled deeper into our sheets, he would begin to sing the woman's song in a lilting, high-pitched voice that would bring the terror and the pity of her plight vividly to life in our childish imaginations. Sometimes he would be reduced to tears as he sang.

I only found out recently that the story Dad told had no connection with the song at all, and it was he alone who was the source of the dark and spooky tale we came to love so much as children. The song's title is 'Come Back Paddy Reilly', and it tells not of a tragedy at sea, but of a wistful longing to return to the lush green beauty of a small Irish town called Ballyjamesduff. It was written in 1912 by a certain Percy French, inspired – rather unromantically – by the emigration to Scotland of a local taxi driver, the man who used to drive the songwriter about town. More prosaic yet, I read that when the song became well known, as it did to all Irish people around the world, the driver disowned the work written in his name. I know, because foolishly, I googled it.

Still, my sister and I adored our father's version. We pictured the low black clouds and felt the rain on our faces; we saw the woman on the lonely strand, looking out to sea, her man lost, her hopes fading and the wind about her howling. And when my father ran out of lyrics and hummed the tune as he backed out of the room, we hunkered down in our beds, glad to be safe from it all.

I wonder what these half-remembered, half-forgotten memories say. Does it matter that Paddy Reilly was not a fisherman but a taxi driver? And what to make of the photographs of me in my football kit, aged ten or so, playing for the football team my father founded and managed, or the shot of my sister held joyfully aloft in his arms, or the one of my parents, smiling and sun-kissed on their loungers in the Bahamas?

Maybe all it says is that we are many different people to the many different people we encounter in our long lives. My father was a protector, a singer of songs, a lover of football, a drinker, a man who raged, a man who was cruel and soft, loving and angry by turns, a man with facets to his nature I have either forgotten or overlooked, or very possibly never knew existed.

Memory is partial, shaded and imperfect. In that sense alone, the past can never be fixed. It shifts and changes shape, it ebbs and flows, morphing like storm clouds over a wild moonlit seascape, obscuring the true horizon, isolating us somewhere on the shore of what's real, alone and calling out our own lament, like the woman in the song.

Neither Paddy Reilly nor my father will ever come home. And yet neither is entirely gone.

We'd elected to leave Dad's ashes in the cupboard in his bedroom for the big day. The green container was unsightly, and putting it on display with the corkboard felt like a step too far. When the ashes first came home, I put the jar on a shelf in the front room, but it didn't feel right. So I moved him into the cupboard, next to a cardboard box holding my maternal grandmother's ashes. My grandmother, too, had found no permanent resting place over the years, condemned instead to accompany me on my peripatetic odyssey through the storms and squalls of life. Which I suppose makes me a bad grandson as well as a bad son.

My sister and I must decide what to do with them both, but we haven't had time. We've said we'll talk about it when she is back in Canada and we have a chance to think about what he might have wanted. He never said.

On my way to bed, I open the cupboard door to see them there, side by side. Dear old Nan never had a kind word to say about my father, and so I can't help but reflect on the quiet harmony that reigns between them in death, so unlike their relationship in life.

The last time I saw my nan alive was Christmas Day ten years ago. She was still living in her own home, but bedridden, hallucinating and in pain. She had developed some particularly ugly bedsores; one where her spine met her hip bones was often an open wound, raw and bloody, right down to the white bone beneath. She could do nothing for herself and spent her days in and out of consciousness, pleading for death.

Nan was deeply Catholic and expected a heaven where a man she had been engaged to – not my grandfather – would be waiting for her. Freddie, a pilot who'd crashed in the desert and died when she was eighteen years old, would come for her in a felucca, a boat common on the River Nile, gorgeous with a single white sail and laden with fruit and flowers.

My grandfather, her husband, had proposed to her at Freddie's grave. He'd told her that if she could learn to love him over time, he would always take care of her and love her in return. He said that if he could swap places with Freddie to prove his love, he would do so. Perhaps out of grief, and after a few weeks had passed, she agreed to marry him, though he wasn't of her class and nor did he have a place in her heart as a lover. She went through with the marriage anyway, to spite her parents as much as anything, and so precipitated well over half a century of unmitigated misery for them both.

She was also superstitious – seeing no contradiction with her Catholic faith – and regularly consulted clairvoyants, one of whom told her that she and I had been lovers in a previous life. I never quite knew what to do with that information.

When I arrived that Christmas Day, the white cat with the rheumy red eyes she'd adopted – or who had adopted her – was sitting on her chest, upright and indifferent to any discomfort she might be causing. The guardrails of the hospital bed were up and the cat looked distinctly territorial. Nan was sleeping and breathing fitfully, not helped by the feline weight on top of her. I picked the cat up and she purred, optimistic for a moment of my attention, until I lowered her to the carpet and she realized she'd been had. She sauntered off to a saucer of crispy brown food and I pulled up a chair to sit by Nan's side and lowered the guardrail.

I took it into my head that, as it was Christmas, and especially given her parlous state, I would try to make our time together extra special, with appeals to her senses and our shared love of all things French. She had attended convent school in France as a young girl. Her mother was French, her father Lebanese. Though she preferred to cling to her French heritage, her olive skin, almond eyes and aquiline nose gave her an exotic, even regal air, and rather undermined her case. Later in life, Edith Piaf spoke to her, as to so many, so I took along a CD of Piaf's hits and put it in the player by her bed. Surely I thought, those subliminal pathways might still be open. I tried to think of smells, sounds and tastes she might recognize or associate with better times and that might encourage her imagination to conjure comforting thoughts and emotions, even through the haze of her evaporating spirit.

I'd stopped at a garage for petrol on the way, and the shop sold dinky quarter-bottles of sparkling wine, so I'd bought one for us to share at her bedside. As she slept on and Piaf told us she had no regrets, I took two dusty crystal sherry glasses to the kitchen and washed them thoroughly, wondering where the cat had got to and whether it had taken the opportunity to sneak back to its resting place on her chest. When I brought the clean glasses back to her bedside, Nan was still sleeping, eyes closed, but her breathing was irregular, as if she were dreaming or disturbed in some way. Perhaps she missed the cat. I opened the bottle, talking to her as if she were awake as I did so, speaking softly so the words might slide into her subconscious. I told her our drinks were poured and waiting. I told her we should imagine we were in a café, in Paris perhaps, and with that idea in mind, I elected to complete the *mise en scène* by lighting a cigarette and blowing smoke in her general direction.

That, it turned out, was a mistake. As the first wisps drifted lazily over her, she began to cough, or rather choke. Gag might be a better word. She had probably not been quite so near smoke for many years, and the effects had caught the back of her throat with a vengeance. I panicked. I stubbed out the cigarette, waved my arms around to dispel the smoke and pushed frantically at the buttons of her electric bed to sit her up and clear her airways. Her face was flushed crimson and her eyes were bulging open with the effort of coughing, and though it didn't occur to me in the heat of the moment, I've since realized she looked very like Edith Piaf in her later years. All I could think about was the consequences of my foolishness.

When the worst of the coughing began to subside, I thought maybe a sip of wine would help. It didn't. I brought water instead. Disaster averted, she recovered, and the coughing had had the unexpected benefit of waking her and making her aware of my presence. We spent a jolly hour together before her carers arrived. I told her tales of her great-grandchildren to try and cheer her up. She didn't say much, except that she wanted to die. I didn't dare tell her how close she'd come. All she asked of me at that last meeting – as she always did when we were alone together – was 'Take care of your mother after I've gone. Do you understand?'

Of course I understood. When you've been lovers in a previous life, there's really no need to explain.

XII

I am making souvlaki, the Greek dish of chicken marinated in garlic and lemon and a whole handful of oregano.

Ellie is coming over this afternoon, and other than care visits, this will be the first time I have had company since the celebration of life. Three weeks on, I am still working my way through the food and drink we ordered for the day, and her help will be much appreciated.

When she arrives, I take her straight round to the back garden. The sun is still hot, but the occasional cloud offers a welcome respite, and in an hour or so it will sink below the ridge of the house. Mum is in her wheelchair under the shade of a small aspen tree. She is wearing only a summer dress, with no blanket to cover her knees, but still she tells me she's too warm when I ask. Even the grass looks dry, and I'm tempted to flick the switch on the fountain's electric motor to send up thin streams of water, just to cool the air close to her. The table is laid for a late lunch and the barbecue is ready to be fired up. I introduce our guest with something inane like 'Ellie has come for lunch', hoping for a reaction but getting not a word in return, not even eye contact.

Ellie does not seem perturbed. She is leaning close to Mum in the wheelchair, but not so close as to be intrusive; you notice these things as a carer.

'Hello, how are you?' she says, pulling up a chair for herself and casually putting a hand on Mum's arm. 'Can I sit here?'

I was ready to guard both women against any awkwardness, but I have clearly underestimated their ability to cope. Both appear perfectly at ease with each other. I offer to take Ellie's bag and the jean jacket she's wearing. The bag is a backpack emblazoned with the Union Jack.

'I see you're flying the flag.'

'What's wrong with that?'

'Nothing at all,' I say, making a mental note to avoid politics, and for good measure, religion too. This is our third social event, if you include the two dates without a spark, so we don't know each other well. Best to tread carefully.

'And a glass of wine, eh?' Ellie says. 'Aren't we lucky? We've got a waiter too!' she adds, and I see Mum is smiling. I have to say, I am impressed.

I bring the wine and two glasses and we settle into garden chairs on either side of Mum. As we talk, I find Ellie's ease is infectious. Mum seems relaxed, even if it is Ellie and I who are doing all the talking, and I begin to relax myself. I give Ellie a rundown on the celebration of life, and tell her that the chicken we're eating today is courtesy of my having ordered far too much for the big day.

'Fine by me. A meal cooked by anyone but me is always welcome.'

Ellie talks easily, flicking her curly hair away from her eyes with one hand, wine glass and cigarette in the other. She is telling us about the hobby she has turned into a business, taking photographs and framing her pictures to sell.

'I get a stall at markets, summer fairs, that sort of thing,' she says. 'I like meeting people and it brings in a bit of cash. Plus, I'm so bored at work …'

She works in marketing and I can imagine she is good at putting the company message across. She is direct and has an enthusiasm that borders on nervous energy. There is little in the way of irony in her worldview, as far as I can tell, and though we are very different creatures, her openness and complete lack of affectation is charming. I can't help but smile.

'What's funny?' she asks.

I'm rescuing the skewered chicken from the barbecue.

'I'm just enjoying your company.'

'Am I talking a lot?'

'Not at all.'

'I'm not the only one; you jabber on yourself, you know.'

'When I can get a word in.'

'Charming. It must be the wine talking. I never usually drink in the day.'

By the time we sit down to eat at the table, we are into a second bottle. I'm offering Mum pitta bread dipped in hummus and tiny pieces of meat from my own plate. She has had a little wine with lemonade, and Ellie is keeping up with me, glass for glass, to the point where I lose all track of time, forgetting the care call until Lisa comes striding around the side of the house.

'There you are. I tried knocking.'

'I'm sorry, I didn't hear anything. Lisa, this is Ellie; Ellie, meet Lisa, our carer in chief.'

Lisa rolls her eyes at my blatant attempt to flatter. 'Don't listen to him.'

An hour later, with the last care call done and Mum sleeping soundly in her bed, Ellie and I are still nattering on in the garden, wrapped up against the falling dew. The longest day of the year was just a week ago, so the sky is still blue, with an early moon that looks transparent.

Ellie has ordered a cab for nine o'clock. It is eight

o'clock now. She has declined my tentative offer to stay over – made out of politeness only – and plans to cycle back for her car in the morning. The second bottle is empty. My mind is turning to the first care call of the morning at seven thirty, and what I can do to cure my hangover. Ellie is apparently undaunted.

I have already been treated to stories of the recent dates she's been on through the Plenty of Fish website. None worked out particularly well. Now she is telling me about Andy, a man she met through her sister-in-law. She is obviously keen. Andy, it turns out, is something of a bicycle fanatic, spending long hours in the saddle when he's not piloting a passenger jet.

'He's away a lot. That would work for me; I like to have my own life.'

'Planning ahead, then?'

'Oh dear, I don't want to spook him. Crikey, he's scared enough as it is, that was obvious last time we met.'

'What happened?'

'Nothing happened. That's just it. We'd been for a meal in a pub and I was hoping he'd invite me back to his for a coffee. Which he did. He was flying the next day and had to get ready, so he suggested I come with him to the bedroom and help him pack. Sounds promising, I thought. He got his case out and laid his uniform on the bed, which only helped in raising the temperature, for me at least. So I asked if I could try it on.'

'The uniform?'

'Yes, the uniform! Well, both senses, I suppose. God knows what I was thinking, because I went to the bathroom and took my top off to put the jacket on. I was still wearing my bra, I'm not completely shameless. Then I did a twirl, you know, thinking I looked quite sexy. I even put the cap on. I mean, he can't have missed the signs. He said I looked nice, so I waited. He did a bit more packing, I waited some more, and then he said he should probably hang the jacket up so it didn't get creased.'

'And then?'

'Then he said he had to get an early night.'

'Any word since?'

'Nothing. Two weeks now.'

'Have you called him?'

'I think I've made my intentions clear. Up to him now.'

'Maybe he's away somewhere. For work.'

'Not according to Facebook he's not.'

I shouldn't laugh, but I do. 'I'm sorry, that's a sad story. Maybe we're all sad stories at this age.'

'It's mad, all this dating stuff. I'm going to stick to my cats. I know they love me.'

'It is mad. Speaking of which, I'd like you to meet Genie.'

'Who's Genie?'

There is just time before the cab arrives for me to find the photograph of Genie on the beach, the one I downloaded from her Guardian Soulmates profile. Ellie takes a long, hard look at the laptop screen and is clearly underwhelmed.

'Yeah, pretty.'

'Pretty? She's beautiful.'

'Oh dear, you're smitten, aren't you?'

She makes it clear she thinks I am crazy to pine over someone I have never met. Headlights beyond the window save me from trying to explain further, to her or to myself.

Ellie has gone, but my headache has not. I've checked on Mum and got myself another glass of iced water as insurance against the inevitable hangover. I should go to bed, but I'm sitting in the kitchen with my laptop open and the photograph of Genie displayed full-size on the screen.

Because now that I'm alone, I wonder. What is it about this particular photo that draws me to it time and again? None of the other photographs in her profile continue to resonate and ripple though my consciousness the way this image of her on the beach does.

Ellie saw nothing special in the photo. Neither my daughter nor my best friend felt as I did, though each subsequently found superficial similarities with my ex-wife and with Marie. And yet it is true to say that when I saw Genie, as portrayed in that one image, I saw someone I felt I *knew*, even though I'd never seen her before.

I acknowledge that previous loves share characteristics with her, just as Phil and my daughter pointed out. Some, but not all. My ex-wife, for instance, has a very similar build, though her hair is curly where Genie's is straight, and their facial features are quite different. Marie is indeed like Genie; the loose hair and the shy smile, the healthy, make-up-free look, these are common traits to both women, I have to admit. And my first love, the Italian beauty, wore cardigans just like Genie's, but is otherwise markedly different.

Maybe my attraction to her has nothing to do with the past and this is a simple case of love at first sight. Apparently, two thirds of us believe it is possible, and I read that of the believers, more than half have experienced falling for someone as soon as they saw them. So I guess I should keep an open mind.

Of course, there's a counter-argument that takes away all the romance and recasts the experience as pure physical attraction. It's a tough one to contradict, given that love and sexual attraction often go hand in hand, so to speak, but it reduces my own experience to something biological and completely devoid of the kind of resonance I felt then, and still feel now.

And is there really any connection between love and lust? Many of us, if pressed, would confess to feelings of lust for members of the opposite sex, or the same sex, who would never make good long-term partners. Lust is not a sign of the potential to love. This debate sometimes breaks down along gender lines. The old adage that men are able to separate the two instincts relatively easily, where women are inclined to find a combination of love and lust more satisfying, persists even today.

And yet love can blossom and grow without lust being involved at all, before lust is involved, and, even more tellingly, when lust is largely a thing of the past. Couples continue to love one another just as passionately and with great commitment even without sex, a situation that may be far more common than we tend to assume.

Around a quarter of carers look after their life partner. Many of those being cared for will have conditions, including dementia, that preclude or inhibit physical love to such a degree as to make it a thing of the past. And yet the care goes on, as does the love, even when the odds are stacked as high as they could be in terms of lust.

So I wonder, beyond her superficial similarities with other loves, beyond the chance that this is love at first sight, or lust at first sight, what are the associations suggested or embodied in that one image? Perhaps our great philosophers have something to teach us. Am I – are we – carrying around a Platonic ideal in our heads and hearts?

What is interesting to me is that Genie chose the photograph as her principal profile image. In her other photographs, she is generally older, more active and pictured against a more exotic landscape. The beach photograph on a grey day is a younger Genie. Perhaps the self she sees in the photograph reminds her of a time and place she longs for or feels a special attachment to? If so, she is having a conversation with herself that I happened to overhear and that resonated with me in rather dramatic fashion as I skimmed the pages of a lonely hearts club.

Thinking about Genie's photo and that sense of familiarity I feel looking at it suddenly brings another image to mind. Although it is now after midnight, and despite my wine headache and dry mouth, I go online, and finally I find what I'm looking for. It's a photograph by Bob Willoughby of Audrey Hepburn.

Genie's photograph and Willoughby's image are virtually indistinguishable, and while any similarity between Genie and Audrey may be mere coincidence, it matters hugely to me, because Audrey Hepburn looks like my mum. And before you say stuff and nonsense, know that I'm not entirely alone in this belief, not simply a fond son wearing rose-coloured spectacles, because others too – carers and relatives, for instance – have said that my dear old mother, now eighty years old and suffering from Parkinson's dementia, was very like Audrey when both were young in the 1950s. You think I exaggerate. And you're right, of course. The truth is, both were much the same age at much the same time when everyone adopted much the same style in hair and make-up and wardrobe. But if I associate my mum with Audrey Hepburn, and in turn associate Audrey Hepburn with Genie, perhaps that's enough to create meaning, and a sense of longing, at least for me.

XIII

It was a day like any other. That was how it felt when I got up around six thirty, showered, made myself a cup of coffee and started to get the medications ready. I could not imagine that by the evening, I would be alone and angry, without being sure who was to blame, but blaming myself.

The first signs something was not right had come the day before. Only I didn't spot the signs. Mum was confused and agitated. When I tried to give her a drink at lunchtime, she gripped my hand hard, digging her nails into the flesh like she meant to hurt. With dementia, you expect mood changes and you can't easily ask for an explanation. When I tried to reason with her, she didn't pay any attention. But then some days are like that.

I thought maybe she hadn't slept well. She didn't want to eat much at suppertime and she was dozy during the evening care call, her limbs more rigid than usual.

Lisa noticed too, but we agreed a good night's rest was probably the best medicine.

The next morning, though, it was hard to wake her. Her eyes blinked open, but it was soon apparent there was a stranger behind them. She'd gone to another place, and I had no idea where that place was. I crushed some paracetamol into her yoghurt with her other medications, just as insurance, hoping for the best.

When Lisa arrived and it came to changing Mum's pad, soaked from the night, the urine was dark brown and smelt strong.

'Probably a UTI,' Lisa said.

Urinary tract infection. Mum had had them before, both when she was with my father and in the care home. UTIs are a normal hazard for older people, especially those who are bedridden or incontinent, or both. But for some reason, I hadn't expected one to happen quite so soon, not on my watch. Maybe I'd done something. Or not done something. But however we had got here, I knew Lisa was right, even though all we had to go on was the urine and Mum's flushed cheeks and confused state. This was different enough from the everyday symptoms of her dementia to merit action.

I called the doctor's surgery to ask for a home visit and Lisa left for her next call. The doctor arrived maybe two hours later. I recognized him, though he was not our usual doctor. He asked me what symptoms I had noticed and scanned a printout he had brought with him of Mum's existing condition and usual medications. She was sleeping as we talked over her, and hard to wake when the doctor asked to listen to her chest, and I had to sit her up in bed. It was difficult to bring her to full consciousness, even more so than it had been earlier, and the rigidness in her limbs had got worse too. The doctor took her blood pressure, then listened to her chest with a stethoscope. He pressed on her tummy with his fingers, asking her if she felt any tenderness, but she was in no state to answer him.

Then he clipped a device to her fingertip with a red digital readout. I asked him what the machine did, and he told me he was checking her blood oxygen levels. We waited and he seemed perplexed.

'Seventy-nine per cent,' he said.

He said that was low, too low, and he took another reading just to be sure. He stood and stared for a moment, then he took Mum's temperature.

'Her temperature is low too,' he said. 'Just a degree or so, but together with the oxygen levels, it could be a problem.'

I asked what kind of problem.

'Sepsis.'

I knew the term had something to do with blood and blood poisoning, but not the precise meaning. He explained that it was an overreaction by the body designed to fight infection. In a healthy person, the immune system was doing the right thing by triggering this response, but with someone like Mum, whose immune system was weakened by her age and her illness, it could be harmful. He said sepsis could lead to organ failure and could happen quite quickly, and that it would be best to call in the paramedics, just to be sure. The hospital doctors could give Mum stronger, more targeted antibiotics, and they could administer the drugs intravenously, something he couldn't do here. He said I should call for the ambulance while he wrote some notes that would go with Mum to the hospital.

The paramedics arrived soon after the doctor left. A young man and a young woman. They were calm, almost nonchalant, in their green uniforms, carrying heavy bags of kit like they had come to fix the plumbing. The woman asked me questions and the man casually toured the house, looking for the best way to get the stretcher in. I heard him whistling at one point. Things had been moving too fast with the doctor's diagnosis. Now I was worried that things were moving too slowly.

When the questions were done, the young woman separated off a yellow sheet from a pink one and said I might want to pack a bag with anything Mum would need in hospital. She listed items that I could have guessed at – nightclothes, toothbrush, slippers – and then her colleague came in and said, 'The conservatory doors look like the best bet,' and they both went for the stretcher.

I found the same shoulder bag I'd used to take things to my father when he was in hospital. It occurred to me that maybe I shouldn't use the same bag because it might bring bad luck, but I knew the thought was absurd. I stood to one side with the bag and a coat for Mum, and watched as the two paramedics shifted her to the stretcher, pulled the metal guardrails up and took her out through the conservatory and down the garden path to the ambulance.

There was a queue to get into the hospital car park. Cars were lined up all the way to the entrance and out onto the main road, just as they were when I used to visit Dad.

I went straight to the accident and emergency reception and said my mother had just been brought in by ambulance. I explained that I needed to be with her because she had dementia and would be unable to communicate for herself, and was likely to be anxious. The receptionist said she would make a note of what I had said and then directed me through the doors to one side of her desk.

Beyond the doors was a ward corridor, and beyond that, another corridor, darker and open at one end to the area where the ambulances parked up. It was like being in a loading bay. Mum was waiting on a hospital gurney. The paramedics were standing by her, clearly impatient at having to hang around, so when I offered to take the paperwork from them and see her through the admission process, they thanked me and were quickly gone. I stood with the overnight bag in one hand, holding my mother's hand with the other, and we waited.

After half an hour, a porter appeared. He looked tired and fed up, but he wheeled Mum expertly through the metal-clad doors to the accident and emergency ward on his own, refusing my help. He left us in a booth with a curtain pulled around, like half a dozen other booths we had passed on the way, some with their curtains open so you could see in, some closed. He left our curtain open. There was a chair in the booth, but because the gurney was set high, if I sat I couldn't see Mum. So I put the bag on the chair and stayed standing.

Her eyes were closed, though she wasn't sleeping, but her lips were moving from time to time and I thought maybe that was a good sign. She felt hot to the touch, even though we had been waiting in the cool corridor, and there was still a distinct red flush to her cheeks and down the side of her neck. I hadn't thought to bring a bottle of water, and I wondered if there was a shop or a machine where I could buy one. Only I didn't want to leave her and I didn't want to miss the doctor.

Forty minutes later, a doctor with a clipboard appeared. She stood in front of us silently, engrossed in her paperwork. She didn't introduce herself.

'Who is this?' she said.

I told her my mother's name. She checked her clipboard again and then let the curtain fall back without a word. Again we waited, until another person with another clipboard appeared. She was harried but not unkind. She asked some questions and filled in a sheet of paper with my answers and said a doctor would examine Mum on the admissions ward shortly. She went away, but reappeared ten minutes later with a porter, who pressed hard on a pedal to release the gurney's brake. We started down the corridor, the nurse leading the way and me trailing Mum on the gurney, bag in hand.

On the admissions ward, there were other people on gurneys. Half an hour passed. Then a doctor came. She was young, smartly dressed and clearly did not have time to waste on bedside manner. She too had questions to ask and more forms to fill in, so she set straight to it.

Name. Date of birth. Marital status. Next of kin. Existing medical conditions. Current medications. Known allergies. Smoker or non-smoker ...

It was the smoking thing that stopped me dead. She repeated the question and I took a deep breath as I shook my head.

'Non-smoker?' she asked again.

'No, I mean, yes. No, she doesn't smoke and she never has smoked, but Doctor, is there any chance these questions can wait? We've been here a long time now. Mum needs a drink, some water, anything.'

'I have to do the form.'

'I appreciate that, but here it is. My mother has had nothing to eat or drink since this morning. The GP said he thought it could be sepsis and ordered an ambulance to come straight away. Yet we've been at the hospital for almost two hours and no one has examined her to confirm the diagnosis. Nothing I tell you about my mother's smoking habits is really going to help. So I'm sorry, but I'm not going to answer any more questions until I get some water for my mother. And I'd like someone to examine her. Now, if possible.'

'You wait,' she said.

Another doctor appeared. He was older, and I suspect more senior. He had a stethoscope around his neck, but no paperwork, and he introduced himself straight away. Calm and in control, he had the courtesy to speak directly to Mum, though she didn't hear him. I told him I was sorry to cause a fuss, but I had to put my mother's interests first. He said not to worry, that we'd get to the questions later, and that a nurse was coming with some water. 'We'll get Mum to a ward and sort the details out later.' I didn't know how I felt about being wrapped up in that 'we', but I think it was meant to be conciliatory.

They put Mum on a regular ward with a saline drip that fed into the back of her wrist. The clear tube leading from the bag of fluid on the metal stand had a green plastic tap, taped to her thin skin.

Six or seven hours after I'd called the doctor, and four hours after Mum arrived at the hospital, she finally looked peaceful, and I wondered if that was because the drip was doing its thing, or because she was dying.

When suppertime came around, the catering trolley parked in the middle of the ward and other visitors began to arrive. I got some help from a nurse to raise the back of the bed, and soon Mum was awake enough to take some juice and a little yoghurt. I looked around at the huddles of family and friends by other beds, their chairs turned to face the patient, all speaking in the same subdued tones to their loved ones and sitting in the same slightly uncomfortable way, attentive but nervous, quick to move aside when a member of staff approached.

Soon they were gone again, and I was the last. With the neon strip lights in the ceiling turned low, only the table lights of the nurses' station offered any illumination, and there was a hush about the main ward, a kind of twilight. Mum was sleeping soundly on her side. I was grateful to have been tolerated for so many hours by the ward nurses, but there was nothing more I could do. It was seven o'clock in the evening. Time to go.

No one had thought to tell me whether she was being treated for sepsis or a UTI, or both.

'Don't worry,' said the night nurse on duty when I asked her. 'She's got an intravenous antibiotic now, and we'll know more when the consultant does his rounds tomorrow.'

'Hey, it's me.'

I call my sister as soon as I get in. I had wondered if I should wait until I had a better prognosis, but that risks being overtaken by events. She has the right to know, and besides, *I* would want to know. Dad died in the same hospital only five months ago, and I can't help but draw parallels.

'What's wrong? Is it Mum?'

I am calling my sister at her work, and that is something I never do. I don't mention sepsis because I don't know exactly what they are treating Mum for, and I don't want my sister to google the term.

'Nothing serious, I promise. A urinary infection, that's all, and you know how common those are. I called the doctor out because she'll need antibiotics, and so she's spending the night in hospital …'

'You mean tonight?'

'Yeah, tonight, I've just come from there. I stayed for supper, it's all good.'

We don't say much more because she has a meeting

to go to, and when I ring off, I wonder if I made the right decision to call. I reassure myself with the idea that if anything serious does go wrong, my sister will not have to deal with the shock of it coming out of the blue. Which now I think about it is not very reassuring at all.

I have sat here in the kitchen night after night, whiling away time, with Mum asleep in her room, but there is a unique quiet to being completely alone here. It's a strange kind of silence, more like a noise you can't hear because it is so constant.

I hate the quiet of this house. I hate it because my father lived here and then died, and because I can't help thinking my mother lived here and that maybe now she is going to die.

I keep telling myself none of this is my fault. I have done my best and these things happen all the time. Just like I told my sister. And even if I could have done more, or prevented this in some way, there is nothing I can do now to save Mum or make her well. She is no longer in my care. She is with professionals who are trained and paid to save lives. And yet they don't know her, and they will not be able to get to know her because the dementia will alienate her from them and them from her. There are other patients to care for and there is the pressure of time and the sheer turnover of staff coming on shift, going off again. Nothing mean or cruel will happen to her there, I know that, and if she needs something, they'll tend to her. If she cries out or pushes the orange button on her handset, they'll go to her. But she won't press the orange button because she doesn't know it's there and doesn't know what it is for. And she won't cry out because she never cries out. But she was sleeping when I left. She sleeps all night here; maybe she will sleep all night there too. And I will go in tomorrow. Early. The nurses won't mind. They let me stay today.

I realize I am angry. But with who? Myself? Them? Fate? This is how the system works. You're home until you're ill, then you're not. You're in hospital with tubes coming out of you. Still, it will be fine. Even if it feels like an affront, like an insult to do this to her, and to me, it's all for the best. This is how it works. I have to get used to it, because this is how it will end one day, sooner or later.

Only not today, not now, please, not so soon.

XIV

If I am at the hospital early, Mum might hardly know I ever left. That is my thinking. I am on a mission now.

I take my place in the queue for the car park, using the outside lane because it moves faster. I know the routines and the rhythms of this place because I used to bring my father to hospital appointments here. Over the last ten years of his life, all his minor ailments seemed to end in one common symptom, namely an inability to drive himself. Taxis were expensive, but he had no hesitation in asking me to make the sixty-mile round trip to drop him, wait, and take him home again. When I could, I did, because it helped to keep the peace and gave me a chance to spend time with my mother. I would stay for a sandwich or a cup of tea and sit with them both in the living room of the bungalow and try to persuade my father to see sense, to get some more help, to be kind and to do some of the chores himself.

My mum's Parkinson's was not as bad then, but still she struggled to manage plates and cups, and struggled even more to tell me how things had been. Sometimes she smiled and sometimes she cried, sometimes both. Back then, I still had hope that everything could be fixed, that reason might prevail, when the truth is the whole fabric of their lives was unravelling.

I can't help but be reminded of his last days as I walk through the same sliding doors of the entrance, pushing the lever on the hand sanitizer and rubbing the thin foam into my hands, negotiating the crowded reception area, checking the charity bookshop for bargains. Mum is on the ground floor, and it takes an effort of will not to take the stairs to the first floor, where Dad died, but to turn left and head towards the far corner of the vast hospital building, turning left into cardiology, G9, the only place they could find a spare bed for her.

I arrive to find a junior nurse giving her water with a teaspoon. I don't immediately know it is water. I have to ask, because the teaspoon holds a little mountain of clear jelly. The nurse explains that the jelly is water with an added thickener to make it easier for Mum to swallow without choking. Mum has her eyes closed and her lips too. The nurse tells me she's been there for an hour or more, trying to get my mother to take the jelly. She doesn't say jelly, she says 'drink', but no one could drink what is on that spoon. The jelly wobbles as the nurse offers it up to my mother's closed lips. I ask her why she is doing this and she says the SALT team – the speech and language therapists – has ordered all fluids to be thickened. She is just doing what she has been told to do.

I notice there are two A4 laminated notices above Mum's bed, one yellow and one pink, both with large printed letters in black. The first says *NIL BY MOUTH*. The second, bizarrely, reads *NO ICE CREAM*. I wonder if there has been a mistake. The wrong patient given the wrong notices. But the nurse says there is no mistake.

She tells me about the test the SALT team use. They put a piece of banana in the patient's mouth and then watch to see if the patient chews and swallows without difficulty. That's what they did with Mum this morning. Only she would not have had much idea where she was, or who these people were, or why they put a bit of banana in her mouth. She has an infection that causes hallucinations and confusion. She is on a saline drip, and if her current state is anything to go by, she was likely barely conscious as the SALT team gathered around her bed like early physicians before the advent of science. She didn't do well with the banana. And because she didn't do well, they said that fluids too might be a problem, and that is why all fluids must now be thickened in order to prevent the patient from choking.

There is worse to come. The young nurse tells me

that if Mum does not take enough food and liquid over the coming twenty-four hours, the SALT team has recommended peg feeding. I know what this is because Lisa has told me about other clients who have a peg feed. I also had to research them when Dad refused to eat and the doctors said they would either use a peg feed or a nasal tube, both liable to cause infection, and with the potential to lead to more problems than they solve, other than keeping the patient from starvation.

A doctor or a surgeon inserts a tube directly into the stomach wall, suitable for pouring liquidized nutrient through, bypassing the mouth and the need to chew or swallow. A tap is fixed to the inserted tube, close to the stomach wall, and another beneath the bag of liquid nutrients. The tap at the stomach wall can be switched off between feeds to help prevent the frequent infections that result from your insides being given a new and direct link to the outside world.

Two days ago, before she was ill, Mum was eating and drinking normally, or as normally as possible given her dysphagia. Her appetite for food, or rather her love of food, has been a characteristic of her hunger for life and a boon to me as her carer. Now, because she has an infection, because she is ill and cannot tell the SALT team differently, because of a piece of banana, they want to take all that away. My mother is listed as a patient with dementia who is likely to experience difficulty

be quite so melodramatic, could I not have said 'I will look at legal avenues' or better still, 'I may be forced to consider my options'? Or perhaps kept my own counsel.

That threat to sue is my father speaking through me. He was forever threatening to sue or bring in the police. He did so with me. I know this because I took a call from a tired-sounding police officer who said I ought to know that my father had made a complaint against me following a letter I had written to him. The police officer had seen a copy and said he believed the matter would fall under the category of family business rather than a full-blown domestic dispute, and then he wished me luck.

It was prompted by a visit I made to the bungalow to find my mother with a back injury sustained in a fall about which my father had done nothing. I called in a doctor and she ended up with a ten-day stay in hospital. When I had settled her at home again, I went to Spain to spend a few days with my elder daughter while my father threatened to sue the hospital for some imaginary crime. I'd had enough.

There is no salutation to the letter. I shouldn't read it again, but I do.

I have to tell you that I regard our relationship as father and son, however fraught and unsatisfactory it may have been for more than a quarter of a century, to be beyond recovery. No doubt you will avoid wanting to hear the reasons why I have taken this decision, nevertheless, here they are for the record:

You have effectively isolated yourself and your wife from all family and friends by your vicious outbursts against others, your consistent bullying of my mother, your mood swings and your drinking, which apparently leads you to conveniently forget the terrible things you've done and said to other people. And now you want to sue the hospital. Your world is fantasy, and dangerous fantasy at that. I frankly fear for her future in your care.

All of this might be forgivable at some level if you had the slightest understanding that you are the author of your own ills. Had you taken the repeated opportunities you've been offered to address your mental state, in particular the anxiety and stress which cause these behaviours, a brighter future might have been possible and we could all get along.

Naturally, I still want to have regular contact with my mother and indeed to see her as often as practicable. I suggest, therefore, you enable her to call me weekly by helping her to dial the number if necessary, and then leaving her alone to speak

freely. As often as I can, I will come up to take
her out for the day or for lunch as appropriate.

I cannot express my utter despair at this
outcome. Not just for your sake, because you
must, in the end, do as you see fit. But for
my mother, I am heartbroken. For over fifty
years, she has loved you faithfully, wholly and
unconditionally. And how have you repaid her?

She is a remarkable woman and when she
is gone, you will miss her more than you can
possibly understand. Make the most of the time
you have left together.

Ask her forgiveness.

I should be thinking about Mum, and yet Dad is cloud-
ing everything. I could use a whole thesaurus to describe
this man; my albatross. The letter reminds me how long
this war has been going on, because I see now it is still
not over. All my life I've wanted to be the light to his
dark, to forge a life of my own as different from his
as possible, and here am I in his house, sleeping in his
bed and living with his wife. More worryingly, here
I am making threats like him, and alone like him … and
talking to him in my head as if he were listening.

Can you hear me from the green jar in the cupboard?
Do you remember calling me to the table and telling
your crap dinner party friends that this was your son, the

only boy capable of coming thirty-second out of a class of thirty-one? Oh, how we laughed. And the stand-up knockdowns on emigration to America, on going to college, on my 'drink problem' as a twenty-year-old? Rich coming from you, who every night nipped at your vodka along with the beer and the Scotch, and then slurred and got angry with my mother or with me, or whoever was to hand.

What I hate most is that it is you I remember, not her. It is your voice I hear, the mid-Atlantic manicured accent: a pleasing gravel to your voice with unctuous overtones, polished up for strangers and pretty women. The shrill renditions of 'Danny Boy' that made you cry long before your audience; the punch or the pinch, meant to hurt because the hug and the kiss were not in your lexicon. I remember your smell, Old Spice, the one I liked best as a tiny child, the one that gave way to Mennen and then Brut. An absurd attempt to bolster your waning sex appeal, was it? And the Tupperware measuring jug, the one you'd requisitioned as your shaving mug, and the little dabs of toilet paper that you stuck to your cheeks with the red dot of blood stemmed, and the styptic stick that made you wince.

I know how you liked your eggs just so, scrambled almost dry – by Mum, never by you – and the white pepper you loaded onto them with the one-handed flip of the pepper shaker, that too made of Tupperware and preserved long after the hinge broke. I remember the Ping putter, your pride and joy, a symbol of your American credentials, one the boys could admire at the local golf club, and envy, and make you feel you'd made it … I remember it all in a way that I don't remember her. Why is it always you I can see in my mind's eye? Why is it me who is here and not you? I wonder, who won the war, Dad, you or me? Who has had the last laugh, the final word? Is this care business, this changing of places, my revenge on you, or yours on me?

And to think that fifty per cent of me is you, and maybe if I'm this angry, I'll soon become a hundred per cent you, a fear that has dogged me all my life. Ours is a banal tale, one that has happened before and will happen again, where the sins of the father fall upon the son. And lest we forget, who was it God the father was content to see die on the cross? Remind me.

Our story and our kind of little war stinks of cliché, stinks of a time and place I've so often tried to leave behind, only to be dragged back again and again. I had thought it was over when you slowly starved yourself to death. But how can it be over when Mum lies in a hospital bed and may never come home, leaving me, not you, to feel the guilt? How can it be over when now I have become the angry man you used to be? I should get away. I should run. I should never have come back.

And yet here I am.

XV

Three days later, I am in a side office at the hospital for the meeting. The room is only just big enough for a desk and a chair, a filing cabinet and a bench seat. There is no window. There are four of them and one of me. The consultant is not the consultant who examined Mum, but a colleague, here simply to sign off on any agreement. He perches on the edge of the desk, casual in a way a judge in a court could never be, and yet that's his role here. The three SALT team members, a boss and two juniors by the look of them, are squeezed onto the bench seat. I get the chair.

There is some chat about a discharge date; maybe even the next day, says the consultant, clearly hoping to ameliorate potential conflict. But there is no mention of the peg-feed dispute, until finally the senior SALT team member plucks up the courage to ask me how I intend to take care of Mum once she's home again.

'Just as I have always done, being careful about what foods to offer her, aiming for as much as I can in terms of quality of life, adjusting what I do and how I do it to the situation and to her needs. By knowing her well.'

They ask me if I understand I am 'feeding at risk'. That is the phrase they use. There is a moment where they wait for me to react to the full impact of the chosen words. I say I do, every day. One of them offers a future scenario involving choking and the effects of dysphagia and the progressive nature of Parkinson's. I say we live and cope with the symptoms on a daily basis, and that while I expect things to get worse, and perhaps even require interventions, we are not there yet.

And when they ask, will I take full responsibility, I say yes, I have until now, so yes. They look at me with a kind of helpless pity. I am unmoved and make no effort to fill the conversational gap. They get me to sign a form indicating that I have been told the potential consequences of feeding at risk, and the meeting is over.

I have phoned my ex-wife to keep her up to date, and spoken to both my daughters. I'm just finishing the evening call with my sister, trying to be quick because she is at work. Having told her about the meeting and claimed it as a victory for common sense, I'm telling her about one of the nurses, Patricia, who seems as concerned with my welfare as she is with Mum's, and keeps encouraging me to go home and rest, promising me Mum will be fine, she'll make sure of that.

'She's right, you'll burn out. You need to take a break before Mum is home again.'

'No, it's all good. Tired, that's all.'

'You sound stressed.'

When I ring off, I sit for a while and just stare. I am at my father's desk in the tiny third bedroom. There is a wardrobe but no bed, a desk and a black office chair, the one I am sitting on now. On the wall is a watercolour print of a green woodpecker perched on a branch with a pine cone hanging beneath, and another print featuring two goldfinches against prickly holly leaves, which for some reason are petrol blue in colour. On the desk is my laptop, with my father's computer pushed to one side, out of the way. The drawers are still full of his stationery and power leads to phones and printers that no longer exist. I have spent long hours here trying to make sense of finances, composing and sending invitations to the celebration, dealing with the probate solicitor, making calls and picking up messages from the landline, but the room – man cave, study, refuge, whatever you want to call it – is still very much his, though the filing cabinet is full of files labelled in my mother's delicate hand. My father's rather fine forward-sloped handwriting is on the Post-it notes stuck under a sheet of plastic designed to protect the surface of the desk, and as always with him, there are plentiful exclamation marks and double underlinings, as if he could shout even on paper.

I can still hear distant echoes of his voice, but I am not angry with him tonight. Or perhaps I am, but I am just too tired to go there. I want to get out of this room, but I am also too tired to stand up.

I need a break, like the hours I used to spend scrolling through dating profiles, often here at this desk. That distraction has gone now and I must content myself with what might have been.

What might have been is still Genie. For some reason, I begin to wonder if the photograph might have a life beyond the dating site. I remember hearing of an image search function, and the thought makes me shift my dead weight in the chair. I open the browser, type in a few words, and there it is, Google Images. I carelessly drop the photo into the search box, like a latter-day toss of a coin into a fountain. To my shock and surprise, up comes precisely the same photograph, unrelated to the dating website and instead associated with a LinkedIn account.

I am completely taken aback. All lethargy has gone, and I am staring at the screen in disbelief. I don't have a clue what to do next. I want to look at the page in question, but I also know this is a gross intrusion, a violation. It's certainly the same person, but this is not the way things should be done.

I click through to her account even as I am debating the pros and cons, my hand having no reservations. And there she is again. Only now she is a real woman, with a real name, a CV, and the hint of a location, courtesy of her current employer.

Even in my weakened state, I can see that what I have already done is wrong. And yet I cannot quite turn away. I am bewildered by the conundrum before me. I am irritated with myself for allowing idle curiosity to put me in this position. Then I hit on an idea. Though my subscription to Soulmates lapsed long ago, I remember there was a period of grace after signing up – a month, I think – a cooling-off period that gave the option of a refund. I also know that the first email in any correspondence will be delivered to the recipient, even if, like Genie, that person does not have a current subscription. Perhaps, just maybe, I could sign up again, send a message confessing to looking her up on LinkedIn and plead for her understanding. I might be able to include my email address in disguised form, but in any case I know LinkedIn keeps a record of those who view a profile, with contact details, and that way she will know who I am.

She might even reply.

XVI

Ten days after Mum's admission to hospital, I am wheeling her down the familiar long corridors in a blue and white wheelchair borrowed at reception. We are on our way to outpatients, where we will wait until hospital transport services tell us they are ready to take her home.

I have given boxes of chocolates to the nurses in a wholly inadequate gesture of thanks for their support. I don't know if there is a campaign group one can join to give nurses more autonomy and responsibility for patients and their well-being, but if there is, count me in. Thanks to Patricia and her colleagues, I have spent less time at Mum's bedside, because she is eating and drinking and growing stronger. The laminated sheets pinned to the wall behind her bed disappeared the day after my meeting with the SALT team and have not reappeared since.

We wait together for about an hour until we are called. Mum and the wheelchair are raised into the patient transport ambulance, and the driver tells me I can take my time getting home because they will stop several times on the way. I watch the ambulance go and retrieve the car from the car park. Driving away is a relief. Mum has not said a word to me today, not even met my gaze, and I have to expect it will take a while for her to recover physically and mentally from the ordeal.

I can't help wondering why this whole process feels like we've been in a war zone. A simple UTI ends with a ten-day stay in hospital, more than enough time for a major operation and a full recovery. In the meeting, the consultant and the SALT team made it perfectly clear that if I chose to take responsibility, I should not complain about the consequences. That is only fair, but also oddly adversarial, considering we are all on the same side here. They are not wrong and I am not right, but it does seem to me that the impetus to escalate interventions, from intravenous antibiotics to peg feeding, is built into the system, a system designed to address acute conditions as quickly and efficiently as possible, leaving very little time to treat people or get to know them. How can a five-minute bedside assessment reveal the person as they were before their illness or who they might be after? Especially when dementia makes real communication difficult, if not impossible, with Mum scarcely knowing where she is or who she is talking to. She has a carer – me – who might be her advocate, but was not consulted at any stage, until I insisted on being involved. I can only ponder with dismay the outcomes for those vulnerable patients who have no advocate, no one who knows them well and who can translate vital background to the professionals calling the shots.

I am relieved my mother is alive, and I dare to believe she will be happy to come home. I am relieved for my own sake too, that I have not killed her within a few months of becoming her carer. But I'm also wary. I know now that I have to be on my guard. There are plenty of experts and support, but the buck stops with me, and it is my job to get the best outcomes for Mum, despite my lack of expertise or training – or, come to that, authority. It's just the way things are.

As we were leaving, a junior nurse mentioned that Mum had dressings on her sacrum – the place where the backbone meets the bottom – because the skin had become fragile, and on her heels, to protect a couple of blisters that had developed. I wasn't unduly concerned. Just one more thing to deal with when we're home, was my only thought at the time, but I said I would be sure to let the district nurses know so they could change the dressings when necessary.

In the afternoon, after the ambulance has dropped Mum home, we take up our usual places side by side under the aspen tree, which has grown surprisingly tall through the spring and summer months. Behind the garden, mature aspens, their leaves with silver undersides, shiver and shimmer in the breeze. I watch them change colour and think of a seascape with light bouncing off water and the swell of waves coming and going. Of course, I should have cut the small aspen down when I first arrived, when it was only six feet tall. My father certainly would have wanted me to, fearful the roots might damage the fountain, but I didn't. It has branches where I can hang birdfeeders that, together with the water from the fountain, create a homespun son et lumière, if you will, designed to engage Mum's interest during the hours she spends sitting here in her wheelchair. But the real reason I love aspens is for their mythological history. They were named by the Greeks to mean 'shield' – the wood is light but strong, and thus perfect for shields. The Latin name, *Populus tremula*, speaks to me now as we both begin our slow recovery from the shock of all that has happened, mother and son, carer and cared for, bandaged in Mum's case, each of us fragile. Though Mum looks calm, I am trembling still, unable to quite relax and accept that the ordeal is over.

Together we comprise something of a tableau ourselves. Were we made of bronze and situated in a town square, there might even be a plaque engraved with the legend *Old Soldiers* to let sightseers know this was a memorial to a long-forgotten war. Or perhaps

I exaggerate. But I think both of us are looking forward to getting the care call over and the day done.

Lisa bowls in, chirpy and obviously pleased to see us again. She is solicitous with Mum and seemingly has an endless supply of chat that serves to bring us back down to earth.

'All right, darling? Come home again, have you? We missed you. Bet you missed us too, eh? I was going to come see you, but you know … Anyway, here I am now, and here you are!'

We will change Mum's pad and put on a T-shirt or nightdress. I have already unpacked the carrier bag full of medications from the hospital, most of which double up on her home meds, and sorted them into piles, and there is also a small stack of dressings we were given to take away with us. I mention these to Lisa just as we're each taking off one of Mum's socks to find that her foot is bandaged from the ankle, with only her blue toes poking out at the end.

'Bloody hell,' says Lisa. 'What's all this?'

'Blisters, apparently.'

'Don't need all that for a blister.'

'And a sore on the sacrum, or so I'm told.'

'Let's have a look.'

We roll Mum from side to side as always, pulling at the institutional knickers that hold the pad in place, down a bit on this side, down more on that, tugging at the trousers as we go and lifting the shirt she is wearing. Mum has her eyes closed, as she often does when being handled like this. Through long experience, it feels to me that she has found, or invented, another place to go that removes her mind at least from the mini-storm, away from being rocked from left to right, hauled up by her arms and stripped of her clothing. It is a strategy I want to remember when my own time comes. We try to ameliorate the indignity of the process with talk and reassurance and jokes where possible, but today I'm short on banter and Lisa is keen to get a good look at the wound on Mum's sacrum.

'A bit more,' she says to me as I hold Mum on her side, and bends lower to examine the dressing. 'Let's just have a little peek.'

I can't see much from where I am on the opposite side of the bed, but I can tell Lisa is peeling back the sticky plaster that I have already noticed is maybe four inches across. I dread to think what it might hide.

'Oh, yeah,' she says, wrinkling her nose in such a way that I get no clue of how bad the sore is.

'What's it like?'

She's frowning. 'You'll need the district nurses in the morning; give the surgery a call tomorrow and ask to be put through to them.'

'Is it bad?'

'Could be worse, I suppose. A couple of centimetres,

maybe three. I think we'll put a fresh dressing on. By rights, I shouldn't really do this.'

'Then maybe we should wait.'

'Be all right. Pass me one of those.'

I retrieve one of the fresh dressings. Lisa tears off the paper wrapping and examines it. 'This ain't the right one.'

I'm too tired for this, caught between my role as so-called principal carer and the reality of my status as a complete novice. 'What do you mean?'

'The Mepore ones are better, easier on the skin.'

'Right. So if it's the wrong dressing and we shouldn't change it anyway, perhaps we should leave this for the DNs?'

Lisa has been applying the dressing anyway, ignoring whatever I have to say. 'There, it's done. I haven't put nothing on it, except the dressing. That'll keep her going for tonight.'

We change the pad and ease Mum forward to slip her nightdress on. Her body is limp and she yields to us in all ways, except for her arms. These she keeps tightly clamped to her sides, and it is a real effort to arrange the nightdress comfortably all round.

'Right, let's have a look at those feet of yours. Honestly, what's all this about?'

The reprise of Lisa's rhetorical question requires no answer from me. I am inclined to jump in and tell her that maybe we should leave well alone, only I still feel I lack the authority to intervene. I hold Mum's left foot six inches above the bed and Lisa begins to unwrap the thick layers of the roller bandage, working her way round the ankle to reveal a bloodied gauze dressing held in place with fawn fabric tape. There is a vaguely hypnotic rhythm to the circular motion of her hands, and I can feel my own fatigue willing my eyes to close. She gathers the bandage in a bundle, pushing it to one side. My mind is just turning to the paper chains we made at Christmas as children when she peels back the gauze to reveal not a blister, but a pink-red wound as big as my mother's heel, ringed by the yellow stain of the blister's fluid, and with a desiccated piece of skin stuck to the dressing.

The wound is not deep, but it is shockingly large. I remember my grandmother's bedsores, and particularly the hole in her sacrum that, in my mind, was a full centimetre deep, with the distinct hint of white tailbone clearly visible beneath the gore. The sight of it still sticks in my memory. This is not like that. There is no bone to see, but I am suddenly heartbroken and destroyed as I try to fight back a rising lump in my throat and tears of shock and sadness.

XVII

I had thought I might find time to continue with the book I was working on in France and care for Mum at the same time. I was wrong. I have tried to write about the experience of care as the days and weeks have gone by, even if it has only been in the form of rough notes and remembered scenes, right up to the hospital stay. But since Mum came home, weeks ago, I have written nothing. I have felt drained of all incentive to relive events on the page. This might be self-pity, but it feels more like despair.

Looking back, it's hard to understand why the experience took so much out of me. After all, I was not the patient. The antibiotics worked. Going in each day to feed and water my mother prevented the doctors fitting a peg feed, and though there were bedsores on her sacrum and her feet had blisters that were open wounds, we came through it.

In the first week or two after her discharge from hospital, the district nurses came twice a day to change the bloody dressings. They went about the task with an easy competence, apparently accepting that hospital could do such things to a vulnerable patient. The routine care visits started up again as if nothing had happened, as did mealtimes and medications. For a while, family solicitations came thick and fast. There were even congratulations from the carers, who seemed to have a new respect for me, or at least to have lost some of their misgivings about a son, a man, in this job. Like the district nurses, they were sanguine about the sores. For many of their clients, a hospital stay signalled the beginning of the end. We were lucky, they said.

I don't feel lucky, except in the sense that we are slowly getting back to where we were before. Something has changed. Not so much in my mother, but in me. She is quieter, more withdrawn, but otherwise as she was, as far as I can tell. But I have a new watchfulness, a distrust of things as they are, a sense that, having suffered one injustice, another could come along at any moment. The system I once saw as a safety net no longer gives me confidence, mainly because there is such a chasm between social care in the community and hospital care. I may be gilding the past, but I have the impression – from my own memories as a sickly child, and from the history books – that in days gone by, that gap was bridged by local district nurses out in the community and by GPs who knew their patients as individuals, who together could spot trouble before it became a serious issue. Now, things are more impersonal and we are all more mobile in our lives, and the minor complaint of a urinary infection or a rattle in the chest can quickly escalate to become life-threatening, a bewildering turn of events that leaves its mark.

For weeks now, I have felt hunted in the day, shattered in the evening and wakeful at night. It is as if I too have lost a layer of skin. Still, we are recovering the status quo. We're no longer an emergency and a source of worry to others, professionals and family. Once again, we've become peripheral, the ticking clock on the mantelpiece of other people's more hectic and chaotic lives, a separate world where no news is good news. Despite my strong sense that our life is more contingent than I fully understood, other people have reverted to seeing us as stable and unchanging. Which, on the surface, is true. The hours are counted out in coffee spoons and cake, pads and medications, shorter days and longer nights.

With the August weather suddenly cooler, threatening an early autumn, the leaves already beginning to show turmeric yellows and paprika reds; with the rain that comes every other day, we spend more time indoors, though we still make forays into the outside world when we can. We wheel down the cul-de-sac towards the village, Mum in the big pink wheelchair, me pushing, taking a long cut past the house my parents used to own before downsizing to the bungalow. We're both still a bit fragile, so often we'll turn around before we reach the house, either at my mother's mumbled request or because I feel I've done my duty and don't want to risk a chill. All of which means our world has shrunk. The tide of life beyond the bungalow has retreated, leaving us not just marooned, but beached.

Now that the memory of the hospital is receding, routine piles the days one on top of another, like bricks in a wall. There is no progression, no recovery, no endgame – none you want to spend much time thinking about, anyway. Maintenance is the key. I'm now an old hand. Minimum effort required because I know what I'm doing. As a result, I'm taking on some authority. I'm certainly better at some tasks, like choosing what to give my mother to eat. Fixed ideas have given way to what works. Ice cream, for instance, helps with dysphagia, despite the hospital specifically banning ice cream when she was there. So in the evenings, pudding might come before cottage pie or pasta with salmon and crème fraiche. In the mornings, I give her yoghurt, pills crushed and mixed in to avoid the chore of taking each one individually, alerting her swallowing response and minimizing her coughing. But if my competence has grown, it is only because I now have a much keener sense of what can go wrong.

When the day is done, I lie in what was once my father's bed and read. If there's no sound of wind or rain and everything is still, I feel like the only living being in the world, despite the fact that I can often hear Mum breathing heavily or snoring from down the hallway. The hollowness I feel during the day is amplified by the stillness of the night.

I have become acutely aware of the inertia of things, the heaviness and immobility of the material world when I feel so alone. Unless I get up and move something, nothing moves. Unless I speak, the house is silent. I don't much like this kind of hyperawareness, where a spider high on the wall or the skin on the back of your hands can become mysterious objects of fascination that might just segue into dreams, or rather nightmares. I know that I need some kind of reflection of self – someone real and present – that isn't this voice in my head. You need that if you're not to lose touch with who you are. At least I do. Because there has been some kind of disconnect between me and myself that I can't quite explain. The public and the private – my appearance to others and the real me inside – are drifting apart: father, carer, son, man, former television producer, former painter and decorator, former … former everything really ... all these incarnations feel like masks I've worn in past performances. Here, there is only one person in the audience, two or three if you include the carers, and no one is paying much attention to my interpretation of the role anyway. The theatre is dark, the auditorium just rows of empty seats. Nevertheless, I've polished up a stoical attitude, not simply because it's required, but because misery is ugly and I prefer to keep a lid on things.

That's the outside. But there's an inside that is worryingly empty, a blank sense of who I am, as if I have been whitewashed and am hard to make out, even to myself. I smile like Frodo, deliver magic pills and potions like Gandalf, but Gollum is always lurking in the shadows. He comes out at night with the spiders. I'm especially aware of him now that I detect a new feeling in myself, a kind of simmering discontent, a nascent sourness I don't want to acknowledge because it sits badly with the selfless suburban hero I have somehow become in the eyes of others – carers, professionals and even my own family. And because there's nothing I can do about it anyway.

So when people call, I have hungry questions. I want the drama of other lives as a distraction. I want to feel involved, especially with those nearest and dearest to me, because caring requires the concentration of so much time and effort on one person, you are also, by default, liable to short-change friends and family. Is there such a thing as carer's guilt?

I have, over the months of caring, shown a reckless disregard for the basics of self-care tantamount to a dereliction of duty. And there are consequences. The nice lady from carers' support tried to warn me about this, but I didn't listen. With Mum's stay in hospital, I have had time to focus on me, and to conduct a full physical, the results of which are both appalling and salutary.

A broadening middle-age spread has crept inexorably towards becoming an obesity issue, albeit localized in a way that makes me appear quite ridiculous, with a rubber ring of fat worn around what I used to think of as my waist. My good intentions to find a sitter and go to the gym – something I have never done before and never had much desire to do – have come to nothing. My excuse, that mirrors and narcissists and tattooed types were unlikely to bolster my self-esteem, was just a smokescreen. Speaking of which, the morning cough has become my stalwart companion throughout the day and impossible to hide from my better self, even as my inner Gollum cradles and strokes the tobacco pouch, whispering to me that to smoke is my consolation, my compensation and my precious. Cigarettes and wine have brought me short-term respite from the daily grind, but at a price that, with age, is proving too expensive for my constitution to bear.

My ills are largely self-inflicted, and might have been overcome by a stronger man, but that does not apply to the latest transformation in my body: skin tags.

There, I've said it. I've managed to speak the actual words, and in doing so put a name to the discovery made when I was in the shower, alone in the house and at my most vulnerable; a condition that I read online amounts to 'small, soft, skin-coloured growths on your skin … that do not usually cause any pain or discomfort'.

And it's true, there is no discomfort – unless I try to pull them off. I swiftly discovered that the dangles are very much part of me, sharing the same nerve endings and blood supply and the same instinct for survival.

Before doing anything that might make the situation worse, I took the precaution of mentioning my condition to Phil over the phone and seeking his view. Other than a rather cagey allusion to the notion that I was not alone, he was keen to change the subject and offered no advice on how to treat the condition. It's odd, given that he takes his own ailments so seriously, that mine are of so little concern. I think he may be spending too much time alone.

So when Ellie popped in for a cup of tea recently, regaling me with stories of two recent dates, one involving a dispute over who would pay for the coffee, and the other a narcissist who asked her nothing about herself, the only thing on my mind was whether I dare broach the subject of my ... tiny dangles. (I just had to find another, more congenial name, something diminutive to lessen my fears.) I made a dash for a gap in the conversation and tentatively asked the question. Were these things normal?

'Loads of people get them, pregnant women for example.'

'But I'm not pregnant.'

'Well, that's something.'

'I think it means I'm going downhill.'

'I think it means you're worrying about nothing.'

'Look, I know it's a big ask, but can I show you? I'd like to be sure they're benign, as it says online, and not something more sinister.'

'Are you serious?'

Ellie needed a cigarette after examining me, but summarily dismissed my fears as baseless. It was an oddly intimate moment – for me, anyway – but she appeared entirely nonplussed. She was still telling me to relax and generally get a grip as she got into her car and drove away.

The National Health Service advised the unusual step of tying off the dangles with dental floss or a length of cotton, but I opted instead for a purpose-made kit that included tiny rubber bands and a plastic tool that allowed me to apply the bands without anyone else's help, thus preserving my privacy at the expense of exhaustive time in the bathroom, multiple expletives and tiny bands pinging off in this direction and that. Finally I became expert enough to perform the application process detailed in the instructions, and if the claims on the packaging are any indication, the bands will slowly strangle the dangles to death.

Minor home surgery is not the only change I have made since Mum has been in the hospital. I have reduced the care calls from four a day to three, and put back the morning call to nine thirty to suit her sleeping habits. She seems to love a lie-in.

I also used the time she was in hospital to rearrange things at home. Mum had ended up in the dining room by default, because her own bedroom was too small for the hoist and I didn't have time to shift my father's bed out of the largest bedroom. I now sleep in one of the smaller rooms, in my father's bed, while Mum's hospital bed is in his old bedroom. I have also taken up the carpet, the better to wheel around wheelchairs and shower chairs and to clean up when necessary. The parquet flooring underneath needs attention, and rogue oblongs of wood keep popping up, only to be replaced like pieces of a jigsaw puzzle. I should glue them down, but I haven't.

As for me, I have decided to cut the wine down to almost nothing, a glass a night, if that. I'm still smoking, but three a day is the maximum, and I am trying to push the first back beyond noon with a view to giving up altogether. And whenever Mum is safely tucked up – early in the morning, or late in the evening – I cycle. I have treated myself to a second-hand bike for forty pounds and have an established route of about seven or eight miles; not far, I know, but enough to get the blood pumping given my level of fitness. I am sleeping better as a result.

The incentive for the health improvements has certainly been self-preservation, but they are also fuelled by a risk I took that could well have backfired, but instead came good. A happy accident, a gift from an otherwise indifferent universe in the form of a message via LinkedIn, though I had not dared to hope, from Genie:

> *Allow me to allay your fears, although your confession did cause me to raise an eyebrow (in particular your admission to finding me via the use of photo match). I found your correspondence to be both charming and amusing. If you were a bona fide stalker you'd be rather hopeless, I'm afraid … I seriously doubt that writing a confession which could later be used by a prosecution team can be of any benefit to real stalkers. We live in an age where information is but a finger-click away if one knows where to*

look. I am not entirely surprised when it is used to the advantage of intelligent people ... and to be honest, I find your efforts flattering, even if a little unusual ...

With tentative contact established, albeit via a circuitous and morally dubious route, I was determined not to put any pressure on her to respond to my intrusion on her life. But I wrote to thank her, and to tell her that I had found her profile while living in France, and that I had now returned to the UK to become a full-time carer for my mother. I wanted to be completely honest about my situation and to acknowledge that meeting in person would be difficult right away. Though if her LinkedIn profile is anything to go by, I suppose I can assume she probably lives in Cornwall, where she works, very nearly two hundred and fifty miles away from the bungalow, so we both have our reasons to be patient and, if she is willing, to get to know each other through writing.

We've now been exchanging emails regularly. I'm finding out more about her life and her as a person. She loves Africa and used to live there, though when I don't know. She has a teenage daughter and is a single mum. She works in admin, but her ambition is to start her own charity to fight illegal poaching of rhinos. I get the sense that she enjoys our contact, but I notice she is always slow to reply, and I wonder if I am expecting too much from a woman I've never met. So I ask the question.

> *Oh bless you! I hope you haven't interpreted my delayed response as a disinclination to continue correspondence. Unfortunately I have very little spare time ... I seldom get home much before seven as I go to the gym after work. Once I do arrive home I'm met with demands for tea; having done my motherly duty and fed my starving progeny I have to clean up the mess (I have no dishwasher) ... do the garden when I can, which is especially vexing now the weather has turned wet and we live on Mud Island.*
>
> *To quickly answer your question, though ... I wasn't brought up in Africa, sadly, but I did live and work there on and off for several years during my twenties. It's the one place that I felt truly at home, where my soul felt peaceful ...*

Genie strikes me as a woman preoccupied with survival: a single mum, busy with work and a teenage daughter, and single-handedly establishing a charity. She is real, and nobody's muse.

I see that now, and I am duly chastened.

XVIII

Uncle Pete, my mother's brother, is arriving for tea. When he offers up the usual plastic carrier bag with bottles of home-made beer and an Australian wine, he stumbles to negotiate the raised threshold of the door and grabs at the hand I offer to steady him. I notice how much he has aged. He is more stooped than I remember, the arch of his once strong back is as high as his head is low, and it is only with a twist of his neck that he raises his eyes to meet mine.

'What's all this?' I ask.

'It's for you, take it, I don't drink any more.'

He is leaning against the wall, unsure where he should be heading and breathing deeply from the effort of getting from the car to here.

'Which way?'

Pete is two years younger than Mum and has always been a robust, energetic man, engaged with all sorts of activities, from his chess club to French classes, from walking holidays to caravanning, making his own beer and wine and always with a hammer or a screwdriver in hand, fitting this to that and repairing anything that needs repair.

In the nearly five months since Mum left the care home, he has visited only three times, excluding the celebration of life. He is only ten miles down the road and he still drives, despite being in his eighties, so I have been a little surprised not to see more of him, though he has phoned from time to time and is always solicitous about Mum and about me. Before I became her carer, he warned me of the burden, but as soon as he realized I had made up my mind, he helped with expenses and offered advice, and it gave me a great sense of security to know he was so close, even if we have not seen much of him.

When we spoke on the phone, he would tell me his own life was very busy, busier than ever, he said. He had something on most days of the week, filling time since his partner died of cancer, and he liked to leave very few gaps in his schedule. Still, I got the impression there was more to his infrequent appearances than pure pressure of time; perhaps something to do with his own health. I know he has had a couple of bad chest infections, but he has always billed them as seasonal and flu-like, bad enough at the time but bound to pass.

Seeing him like this, I wonder, and I hope he doesn't register my concern.

He kisses Mum on the forehead, pats her arm and calls her 'old girl'. She doesn't respond or seem to recognize him, and he retreats to the sofa. I always try to leave Pete and Mum alone, so I make tea and take my time, hoping Mum will benefit from one-to-one contact with her brother. They have a vast hinterland of experience in common: from their childhood in Egypt to forming their own families at similar times; from living close to each other at various stages of their lives to sharing responsibility for their mother in later years.

When I return with the tea, I find them sitting in silence; not an awkward silence, but something connected, like two people waiting for the same bus. I get the sense Pete finds seeing Mum difficult. I noticed at the celebration of life that there was an element of reserve in his demeanour with her, a sense of deep compassion, but from a distance, close but not too close.

I am sure that it is hard to see your sister in a wheelchair, ageing and only partially able to share her feelings with you or hold a conversation. I am sure, too, that when a sibling declines so tangibly, there is always the thought that you are every bit as vulnerable. Ageing may not be contagious, but fear of ageing might very well be. Mortality is the elephant in the room as we take tea and cake, but we're all used to its presence.

Today, I have an agenda. I want to ask Pete about the past, and about Mum in particular. These two people whom I have known all my life knew each other long before me. Together they have made the journey from a place I know little about, to here. Pete may have stories to tell about Mum. The chance to hear about her life before me is an exhilarating thought. I have some photographs of that time in albums, but no memories to interpret them and weave them together. And without in any way wishing to cast a pall on proceedings, the wormhole my uncle can pilot for me will only remain open for as long as he continues to live well. So, with Mum taking a nap in bed after the lunchtime care call, now seems as good a time as any. When I ask, he says, 'Only too happy, but before I do, I've got news for you.'

'What's that, then?'

'I'm moving to Devon. There it is, I've decided.'

Two of his three boys live in Devon, grown and with families of their own, as does his ex-wife. There is every reason to be closer to them.

'About time,' I say, though the truth is, I am intrigued about the precise motive. I know that over the last three years, he and his ex-wife Ann have been spending more and more time together, and I have my suspicions. 'Go on.'

'I've thought it over carefully …'

'Very carefully, I'd say. You've been on your own for

how long now?'

'Hazel died ten years ago.'

Hazel was Pete's partner for almost thirty years after his divorce from Ann. Since her death, Pete has spent more time with his boys, often meeting up with his ex-wife, and with both of them now in their eighties, it has been clear for a while that any bitterness or rancour over the past has long been put to one side. More than that, it seems they have managed to form a new relationship, though I can only guess at how far things have gone.

'The boys have been on at me to move down to be closer to them for a couple of years. I think the time has come.'

'And Ann?'

Pete smiles. We both know something significant has happened and I want to know more.

'Well, years ago, we had a hard time, but that's all forgotten now. We enjoy each other's company. Truth is, I think we're in love. Again. In fact, I don't know that we were ever out of love. Only I'm not moving straight in with her, I've said that to her and the boys. I don't want to cramp her style. She's got her dancing and her own friends. We'll just take it very slowly.'

They've been apart almost forty years. They are approaching the end of their lives and they want to be together. Simple, and yet a miracle in its own way. Pete has found his travelling companion for the road ahead, and so has Ann. Perhaps they were walking alongside each other all along, but unaware of the other feeling the same way. Now they know it and so does everyone else. Theirs is a true love story.

I want to hug him. Instead, I use words he uses all the time to tell him how I feel about the news, 'fantastic' and 'fabulous' and 'lovely', and I say I couldn't be happier for him, and for Ann. And because I sound sentimental, I add that I'll be glad to see the back of him.

'Good for you,' he says. 'So let's talk about your mother.'

I ask what she was like before meeting Dad, because that's what I really want to know. Who would she have been if they had never met? What did she want for herself with her whole life ahead of her?

'She was rotten at sports, I remember that, where us boys were competitive in everything. But I can remember her getting prizes on prize day and I never even bothered to ask what they were for. She deserved more recognition. She loved horses and she was a bloody good horsewoman. But I never heard her say "I want to be a secretary", even when she went to secretarial college, and she never said she wanted to be a hostess in the airlines, even when she got the job. It was just a job.

'We had a house on the edge of the desert in Egypt and our parents would go horse riding every morning and dancing every night, often until dawn, when they'd come home and change their clothes and head off to work. You have to remember this was wartime, the 1940s. There were soldiers coming and going, some billeted with us, a bored civil service that was part of the British Army. There was an English club with wonderful dances, big bands and a lot of drinking. I remember stories of people being so drunk they would shoot the light bulbs out rather than get out of bed to turn them off.

'Your mum was one of a trio of older girls, together with her friends Bonnie and Bubbles. Frances was her real name, but she was always Bubbles back then. When they were at the house, it was "Pete, don't do this, don't do that …" She was often the one looking after us when nobody else was home. And quite often, a lot of the time, we were there on our own, just your mum and us, and Badir, the housekeeper. When your grandparents were home, well, there was another war going on between them, quite openly and for all to hear. Your grandfather Gangi was quiet and calm, but your grandmother had a flaring temper and she controlled your mum, trying to get her onside for the rows. I wonder now how much … what's the word … training your mum had in her teenage years. I think she made up her mind she was not going to let that kind of conflict happen in her own marriage.'

'Did she have boyfriends when she was young?'

'She was *so* popular, especially with the boys, and she

was very good-looking. They'd come to me and ask about her, but we were all innocents in those days and she never mentioned a love life, even if she had one, which I doubt. The first time I saw her smitten was with your dad, and she was absolutely wildly, madly in love with him. Your dad was eloquent, adventurous and Irish, and your mum had no chance. The marriage went ahead, and the night of the wedding, we were all sleeping downstairs on the floor, and I remember going into your mum's bedroom the next morning and seeing the two of them cuddling up in bed. I looked at them and I thought, yeah, you're good together. That's true love, I thought. It was a love that later your mum and dad spoiled, but he was her life and that was always true from the moment they met. She did things his way, she went for jobs he suggested, and she was submissive, willingly and lovingly, but she knew how to keep hold of the strings, quietly in the background.

'Your grandmother never had a good word to say about your father, but I talked to him over the years about family, philosophy, kids, marriage, lots of things, and I know he loved your mum too, just as much as she loved him.'

Later, with Pete gone, I sit next to Mum, who is having supper in bed. We've got a bowl of mint choc chip ice cream and it's going down well. Each time I give Mum ice cream, I think of that laminated sign on the wall above her hospital bed, *NO ICE CREAM*, and take a moment's satisfaction.

I'm recounting the story of Uncle Pete and Ann getting back together after so long. Mum responds from time to time with 'Mmm'. I've noticed that certain names – Ann, for instance – will often spark a look of recognition on her face. But I get the feeling I should not judge what she understands from the way she responds. In the same way that her legs scarcely move because motor functions are an effort to organize, it seems to me the dementia causes her to feel no social pressure to react to information. None of which means she is not hearing and understanding what is being said, or processing the news to add to her stock of memories and thoughts.

This is a good time of day for us to chat. In the afternoons, she often experiences a mood dip and it's not uncommon to find her glowering and pulling at invisible threads in front of her, resentful of any interruption. By early evening, her spirits usually brighten and we can share a joke or pretend to spy on the neighbours through her bedroom window, or talk about the past. It is clear she sees no impediment to a bit of cheeky banter. At times, she can be positively coquettish, particularly if my sister or my daughters, or one of the carers, are here with us. If others laugh, she laughs along, her social brain fabulously alive to the nuances of interaction with others, to manners and humour, to subtext and irony.

These 'sweet spots' – another is first thing in the morning after juice and yoghurt – have, I am pretty sure, a literal cause. Sugar. It is a standing joke between us as to whether her tea has enough sugar, or any at all. I am torn between the look of distaste on her face when I try to fob her off with just one spoonful and an instinct that tells me her body is calling the shots and must have good reason for demanding quite so much sweet stuff.

By seven o'clock, the sugar high fades as quickly as it came, and if I leave her for a while to go and clear the kitchen or prepare my own supper, I can return to find her, head bowed, beginning to doze. I press the button on the electric bed to lower the mattress, position her pillows, give a gentle tug on the slide sheet to shift her onto her side, place another pillow behind her to support her, a smaller one between her legs to prevent one knee slipping behind the other and straining her hips, and another under the other knee to support both legs. I tuck her up, lower the bed, place crash mats on either side – not that she has ever come remotely close to falling out – kiss her on the temple, stroke her head and sometimes scratch her scalp or rub her back, put out the light and say goodnight. Her eyes close and she can be asleep before I leave the room. I consider myself the most fortunate of carers because she will often sleep right through until seven the following morning. If she does wake, turning her pillow or stroking her head will often send her straight back to sleep. I know others have it so much harder; their daily care stretches into the night with no beginning and no end.

I make supper for myself from the leftovers of Mum's cottage pie – a ready meal, I am embarrassed to admit – supplemented by cheese and crackers and a glass of white at the dining room table, where I am surrounded by piles of old photographs and ragged albums, none in any kind of order. There was no time for Uncle Pete to wade through them with me, but I want to see if I can match the black-and-white images to his take on Mum's early years, especially her youth in Egypt. Because I am perplexed. Uncle Pete answered my questions, told me some things I didn't know, along with many I did, but I am not sure I gained any real insight into Mum.

I am drawn to the romance, and indeed the order, of the early albums. They are of a different era, when the people collating the photographs took the time to write names and dates underneath them. Rice paper separates the graphite-black card pages. The prints are small and I have to peer closely to make out who is who. I see the captions are in Mum's hand, and I feel a little stab of emotion when I read the 'me' in *Bubbles, Bonnie and Me, Heliopolis, 1949*. Mum is beautiful, and though beauty is not a virtue, it is a quality somehow marvellous to behold in one's mother. But I could easily apply the same judgement to all the young folk in these photographs. It is their youth that is beautiful, the vitality in their expectant faces, the optimism implied by so much life ahead and so little behind. The innocence of a time before social media. A time that is now part of a wider history and an era that is long gone.

I turn to my parents' wedding album, white and padded with a sleeve of the same material to protect the contents, to find Mum laughing and happy, her face fresh and her hair apparently jet black, her trademark winged front teeth recognisable. Dad is skinny, more Irish than I remember him, with angles to his face and forehead and neck, all definition; handsome, striking even. They are twenty-three years old.

I go back to the Egypt album and realize there are pictures of my sister and me towards the back. I must be five, my sister three. The captions say *Beirut*, again in Mum's hand, but I have no memory of the trip to Lebanon and it is too late to ask anyone about it now. Even the colour images I stumble across are hard to place until we get to our first house near Heathrow Airport, to the west of London.

There is one of Mum, dressed in the style of the late sixties and early seventies: a polo-neck sweater, a shorter skirt, her hair more feathered, off the ears and longer at the back. The sight of her reminds me of my own burning desire for long hair at that time and my father fighting me all the way. All the boys wanted the same, to be like George Best, Geoff Hurst and Ray Clemence, our footballing heroes, with their hair 'halfway down their backs'. Football reminds me of the nights kicking a ball around until it was too dark to see, until the distant voices of our mothers calling us to come home could no longer be ignored.

I push to one side the photos of my parents on holiday. I have seen them before. Images of Dad pretending to hold up a palm tree that leans precariously to one side, broad around his middle as I am now, his forehead taking up more real estate than his hair, just like me. My mother is still beautiful, always smiling, chubbier but making the most of it, squeezed into a bikini, sunglasses big like the eyes of flies. Then the two of them side by side on sunloungers; another of Mum in a shimmering long dress for a 'do'. Here and there I see two teenagers – my sister and me – scowling or posing, grumpy or slumped. Happy times.

There is a plastic bag of I-don't-know-what that turns out to be envelopes in clear covers produced by the Philatelic Club of the airline BOAC. Each certifies the bearer to have flown on an inaugural flight aboard a 747 or Concorde, from here to there on this date or that, with details of the crew and the flying time and the route. They might be of interest to someone, an aircraft enthusiast perhaps, but I don't feel the need to preserve them, and I am just wondering what to do with this collection when I come across a series of letters, all in the same distinct and familiar handwriting.

There are eight in total. Each one is addressed to my mother in her maiden name. They are dated from May to June 1957, and cover the weeks leading up to my parents' marriage on June 29th, written when they were separated because my father was posted to work in Luxembourg and my mother was at home in England. All the letters are in my father's archaic and graceful forward-sloping hand, and are stamped Luxembourg-Ville. None from my mother to my father have survived. I wonder what they are doing lumped together with the airline envelopes, until I realize all bar one has had the stamp torn away, presumably to add to a collection. Was my father a philatelist, I wonder. If so, I never knew.

I pull out the first letter, written on both sides of the blue paper, airmail weight with an onion-skin quality to it. The ink is blue too, from a fountain pen, and the words on the page have not faded very much in the intervening half-century. The letter is dated Sunday 19 May, 2030 hours, using the twenty-four-hour clock he would have been familiar with from his work at the airport, flight-planning DC-6s and DC-4s. There is an address, and when I check it out on Google Maps, I find a four-storey building, apparently an infill to a block that might be from the 1930s. But for now, my whole attention is taken by my father's words written to my mother:

> *My Dear Little Pud,*
>
> *It was very nice to hear your voice and to hear you laugh the other night, and it made me wish you were here … I know things have been hard, but I do love you in every way, and very soon I shall prove this to you. You are my friend and my lover …*

He goes on to reassure her with tender words and promises that they will be together soon, and says they will be happy together for the rest of their lives. In other letters, he apologizes for being absent and leaving the wedding arrangements to her. It is clear how much he misses her and it is just possible to read between the lines and to understand how much she misses him too.

Uncle Pete's words are echoing in my head: *He loved her too, just as much as she loved him.*

Five weeks after this letter was written, they were married. They took their honeymoon in Paris en route to Luxembourg and 32 Rue Arthur Herchen, where only a few months later, they would conceive a child.

Me.

XIX

It's the last care call of the day. Zlatica has just arrived. She is Slovakian by birth, married to a Brit, with two children, both boys. She's also a qualified chemist, though she can't practise in the UK and so works as a carer. She has been doing the job for four years and manages to always be jolly, even when I suspect she's not feeling jolly inside. Which makes her rather marvellous in my eyes.

It only takes a few minutes to get Mum ready for bed; Zlatica and I are pretty good at the routine now. After the change of pad, the application of creams and powder and a hairbrush for Mum, we sit in the kitchen and Zlatica fills in 'the book' while I get supper ready. This is a folder with pages for medications, bowel movements, and the time the carer arrives and leaves, and there's a space for Zlatica to write what we did, how Mum was, and so on.

Keeping records is an important part of the job for all the carers. It protects Mum and them – and me, I suppose. Because there's always a written record to refer to if any problems arise. As a safeguard and an insurance policy it may be partial, but it's all we have. I don't keep a record myself. I don't think I could bear it. Living the day is enough.

It's been a long day today and I'm exhausted, but with Zlatica gone and Mum sleeping peacefully, the house is quiet and there is time to think. I'm conscious of the days and weeks and months to come. Like the horizon, although I can only see so far, I know there's an ocean of the same beyond. My role as carer to my mother is not a sprint, but a marathon, and I fully recognize I've only just got into my stride. Mum's doing well and I get compliments on her well-being, but I know I will finally be judged on her longevity and my ability to stay the course.

I am, after all, totally responsible for another life. A single parent to my own single parent. And that, as the young folk have it, is awesome. The first few nights – the first couple of weeks actually – I would lie awake with my door open, and hers, and I'd listen and hear nothing and wonder … is that good or bad? Is she alive or dead? Am I really cut out for this? What if I get it wrong? What if all those warnings turn out to be right? I'm learning, but I'm still a beginner in care, basically without a clue. Which is why there's a formal – and informal – monitoring system that serves to protect vulnerable people like my mother.

At first, I wasn't really conscious of being watched. But as the days and weeks have gone by, I've become more aware that being seen to do the right thing is a vital element of the job, almost as important as actually doing the right thing. Though opinion varies on exactly what the right thing is. For instance, district nurses have a professional responsibility with regard to how medications are administered. Because Mum has trouble swallowing, the Parkinson's nurse, Sylvia, has sanctioned crushing the sixteen pills she has to take each day and mixing them with yoghurt or ice cream. When I told one of the district nurses what I was doing, she grimaced and suggested I might want to get that in writing.

The carers are not permitted to administer medications in 'disguised form' – as they call it – under any circumstances, even with a letter, and you can see why such prohibitions are necessary. So I give Mum all her meds and take responsibility for the way I do it, and so far things are working okay.

In truth, I'm an amateur working with professional management. Most unpaid carers are relatives like me: sons and daughters, parents or spouses. None are trained for the job before taking it on. All have lives of their own, including work outside the home, and other key family members or partners who call on their time. Many, those of a certain age especially, have their own health conditions to cope with. In the literature given to me, I read that 65 per cent of carers over the age of sixty have health problems or a disability, and that nearly 70 per cent say being a carer has an adverse effect on their mental health. Statistics vary, but according to Carers UK, there are more than seven million carers in the UK – that is one in ten people – which, when you think about it, means there are a huge number of ordinary folk performing extraordinary feats of love and care every single day, and paying an enormous price themselves. Shocking, really.

The statistics provide urgent reasons for the state to offer support in every possible way, from physical assistance to emotional backup, education, training and even financial incentives. But this side of things, as I am beginning to understand, is less of a priority than it might be, simply because it costs money. When people are caring for relatives and partners because their duty of care is based on love, successive governments have felt it prudent to avoid any disruption to that vocation by introducing incentives into the equation.

I've started thinking again about my own needs. In earnest.

If I'm not to go crazy in suburbia, hemmed in by plastic windows and little red Hondas and the company of strangers in uniform, my life must be augmented with some quality 'me' stuff. The question is, what or who?

I took down my Plenty of Fish profile long ago. It's true to say life is a bit flat. And while Genie and I have exchanged the odd email, she is clearly preoccupied with her own life, and it is not as if I can take time out, even to meet for the first time. I must learn acceptance, and I suppose I had fun trying. The fishing filled some long evenings, and Ellie's friendship is a bonus.

Still, a window on the possible has been tightly slammed shut, and for good reason. It was all a fantasy and there's no point in tormenting myself with such things any longer. I feel grief too. Not only is my labour to find love lost, but I have to recognize that in very sensibly giving up the quest for a latter-day Beatrice, I am, of necessity, condemning myself to celibacy too. A potentially lethal capitulation, marking the beginning of the end of something. Middle age segueing into old age, love seeping away forever.

In *One Hundred Years of Solitude*, Gabriel García Márquez wrote that 'Sex is the consolation you have when you can't have love.' Okay, Gabriel, I'm with you, because I think I might be doomed to see out my days in solitude. Must I cease to hope? Or live on in desire? And where the hell is my consolation?

Like Theresa, the lovely Irish lady from the care home, I feel like shouting out to anyone who'll listen, 'Nurse, Nurse, what should I be doing?'

Only no one is listening, and if they were, a middle-aged carer suffering pangs of sexual desire, and worse still, bewailing his lot publicly, is unsavoury; quite enough to earn a place in the second circle of hell, reserved for the lustful, where Dante tells us we're going to be buffeted by terrible winds and violent storms.

There's only one person who might sympathize with my plight, so I call him.

'I've got bad news, or maybe good news. I'm going to hell.'

'That is not news, dear,' Phil says, 'but tell me more.'

I don't know when we started calling each other 'dear' and 'darling', but it may have been when we lived together in France and the locals came to their own conclusions about our relationship. It seemed churlish not to play up to the part.

'The upside is that Cleopatra, Dido and Helen of Troy are waiting to welcome me there, condemned by their own queenly lust.'

'Yes, though I wouldn't expect too much of a fanfare. So tell me, how are you really?'

XX

'Daddy!' Two voices chorus my favourite word in the English language, heralding the arrival of my daughters, accompanied by Maisie the dog, her rear end lurching from side to side, powered by her wagging tail, little drips of wee on the carpet confirmation of her delight at seeing me again.

Today is actually all about me, and legitimately so. It is my birthday, and my children, who are now adult women of twenty-two and twenty-six, have come for lunch. They may well be bearing gifts, to judge by the carrier bags stuffed with things all wrapped up and the bottle of red wine the elder is holding as we hug and kiss.

I feel the object of unconditional love, in stereo today, with Maisie as the boom box. It is entirely possible I am exaggerating, or even delusional. Certainly, I'm told this kind of connection with one's offspring is rare. We're used to physical separation from my time in France and from their time at college, but we're also used to being together, just the three of us, four if you include Maisie, and we do, always. Now that I'm Mum's carer, we are geographically closer than we have been for a year or more, but still it has been a while since we have sat down together, and so we have another reason to celebrate.

I am making chilli with rice, a favourite. While I cook in the kitchen, with Maisie keeping an eye on my every move, the girls sit with their grandmother in the conservatory. They each have a glass of Prosecco, and I've poured a small one for Mum mixed with a little lemonade. It is interesting to see them together. Mum likes company, always assuming she is not tired, but I think she especially likes the company of young women prone to smiles and laughter. She seems to find the joy infectious, and the girls lavish attention on her and tell stories they know may not be understood entirely, but that have the rhythm of a beginning, middle and end, and thus an arc Mum can follow – or so it appears.

We tell more stories as we eat and as I feed Mum little forkfuls from my plate. Maisie is still staring at me earnestly, and I'm feeding her too. She is looking older, with every reason now as she is thirteen. 'Pup', as we often call her, has been a constant in all our lives from when the girls were children, through separation and divorce. As a puppy, she slept in the storeroom of the off-licence where I worked, and sat at the bottom of the ladder when

I was a painter and decorator. She moved backwards and forwards between my ex and me, but was always there in the scene somewhere, like a painter's motif. I miss her. I would like her to be here with me and Mum, but that won't happen.

My elder daughter is completing a Master of Science in global nutrition, a surprising choice as she studied languages for her degree. She is in the middle of writing a dissertation and is worn out. Her natural diligence, and a sense that she has something to prove having come from an arts background, means she puts in long hours. Her skin is pale, more so than usual, and being a good dad, I tell her so.

'Thanks for that. I know, but there's so much to do.'

'Tell me again when it's due?'

'Four weeks, three days.'

'Not that you're counting. Anything I can do?'

'Read it for me? Pray?'

'It'll be fine. How's your man?'

'Lonely, I imagine, like me. We live together but seldom meet. He's working hard too.'

Her boyfriend works at the sharp end of nutrition, having recently started up his own catering company. They're good together; there have even been vague hints about starting a family, but that may have to wait, by the sound of things.

The younger recently completed her degree in drama

and is working at a hotel health spa within walking distance of the family house in my old home town. She is trying to pay off her college overdraft on minimum wage, handing out towels to middle-class ladies who like to complain before they swim or get a massage, and not having a lot of fun. She is low, too, because we were told only a few months ago that she needs a new hip. This has long been an issue. It started when she was eleven or twelve with a growing spurt that seemed to leave her with one leg longer than the other, or that was what the GP said, but specialist after specialist had their own diagnosis, including childhood arthritis, a tilted pelvis and Perthes' disease, the latter likely to see her in a wheelchair by the age of eighteen. We were lucky that particular diagnosis was wrong. She had learned to live with a hip that did not work as it should until the pain returned with a vengeance only recently, and an X-ray revealed the bone was disintegrating.

I have tried to be there for appointments and done everything I can to find an alternative treatment, something that would not mean a young woman who loves to dance could no longer run or jump without fearing the consequences. Since I've been back from France, we think we have finally found an experimental procedure that just might work. She is now enrolled on a programme to resurface the hip joint with ceramic material, so it's just a question of waiting a couple of months for the operation. That is scary and exciting for all of us, but mostly scary, and she is being fabulously brave.

One of the frustrations of being a carer is that my time is not my own and there's no day off. There is a background hum of fear that I can no longer dedicate my attention to my daughters in quite the same way I once could. Given how intertwined our lives have always been, that might be a relief to them, but I don't think so. It's certainly not for me. Even when I was in France, we saw each other every couple of months. I was able to research doctors and surgeons and help my elder daughter with her studies, and we spent holidays together two or three times over the year. Now, I can listen and offer advice, but I can't be of much practical help. I earn nothing. I can't be there for the event, or pay the fees, or drive them to the interview or the appointment. Not that they ask any of these things of me, but I am acutely aware that time is going by and stuff is happening, to them and to me, albeit remotely from each other. I miss being more involved and more available. There's loss in that, especially if, like me, you aspire to the condition of a doting dad.

'Oh, I forgot to tell you,' says the younger. 'Guess who came into the spa?'

'Who?'

'Marie.'

I am taken aback, though I have no reason to be

surprised that my daughter and my ex-girlfriend – partner, whatever the right word is – might bump into one another. After all, Marie works close to my former home town and lives nearby, though no longer in the house we once shared. To hear her name again brings the past rushing back when I have tried so hard not to think about all that. I want to know more, and yet I don't want to know, and my daughter can sense the dilemma.

'I did wonder if I should mention it.'

'I'm glad you did. But Marie's not a spa type.'

'I know. She was there with a girlfriend, probably one of our gift-voucher days or something.'

'How was she?'

'Okay, I think. She didn't notice me at first, so I went over and said hello. She looked the same, though her hair is shorter. I'd forgotten how pretty she is.'

I haven't forgotten. 'Did she say anything?'

'She was sweet. It took her a moment to recognize it was me. Actually, she started crying.'

'She did?'

'She said she still misses you and thinks of you.'

I'm too bewildered to reply.

'Don't worry, Dad, she said she was happy too. She's a grandmother now.'

The girls have gone and taken Pup with them. Mum is sleeping and I am sitting with my knees up in bed and staring at the screen of my mobile phone. I am also drunk. Really quite drunk, in a way that a carer with responsibilities should not be drunk.

It is almost ten o'clock, but it is still my birthday. I've had presents from my daughters and from my ex-wife. A card arrived in the post yesterday from my friend Jojo. And my sister called this evening when the girls were still here and we had a jolly time handing the phone around between us before they left to go back to their mother's house, my old home.

The good news is that in taking myself to bed, I have stopped drinking. I have a large glass of water loaded with ice, moisture condensing to form a little puddle on the pine bedside cabinet. The curtains are closed and I am lying on the left-hand side of my father's bed, still allowing a little space for his ghostly outline. I am trying not to think about him or his nights alone in this house, and trying not to see the parallels now that I am here, every bit as isolated as he once was.

I'm thinking about Marie, about when she came to visit me in France. Far away from home and our responsibilities there, we had a golden couple of weeks, swimming naked in the cool waters of the Vidourle and the Vis, gorging on the late-summer fruits of a love that had been battered by the elements but could still taste sweet as ever.

For a brief while, I believed we might make it, or wanted to believe. All doubts, I kept to myself. The proviso Marie set was that we keep the rekindling of our love a secret. Her mother in particular had never been my greatest fan. Still, we clung to each other, until a couple of months of desultory Skype conversations and pathetic attempts to hide the evidence of our relationship from her children, and especially her mother, undermined any lingering hope in me, and with a heavy heart, and after a long cycle ride through the black vines and many hours sitting at the same swimming hole where we had swum together, I wrote a Dear John letter.

Marie immediately cut off all contact with me. She needed to protect herself, she said. We have not seen each other, nor spoken or even written since, and now, because of a chance meeting in a hotel spa, here I am, tipsy and staring at the screen of my phone, rereading my text message before I press send because I know I am drunk and I know this is the wrong thing to do:

I hope you won't mind me wishing myself a happy birthday from you. The girls were here today and send their love. I do too.

Then, as you do when self-pity is liberated by alcohol, I pressed send. Miracle of miracles, ten minutes later, I got a one-liner back with the words *Happy birthday*, but no kiss.

Still, I fell asleep feeling oddly buoyed and no longer quite so alone, though it was perfectly clear Marie was only being polite.

AUTUMN

XXI

There is a poem, much loved by anyone who knows Thomas Hardy's work, a poem I have been thinking of these last few days. It's called 'The Voice', and it begins like this: *Woman much missed, how you call to me, call to me …*

The poem is one of a series that Hardy wrote to his wife after her death, despite the fact that their marriage was not a happy one. Emma lived out her last years alone in the attic of their house – her sanctuary and refuge, she called it – and Hardy took lovers.

It is the last stanza that I hear in my head as the season changes and the days grow shorter, mostly because it speaks to the journey I am on with Mum:

Thus I; faltering forward
Leaves around me falling,
Wind oozing thin through the thorn from norward,
And the woman calling.

I am faltering less than I did in the beginning, but there is a melancholy to the lines that is undeniably part of our shared experience together. Our autumn and the season's display in the garden – the chameleon colour changes of the trees, branches growing bare in the wind – together encourage a state of reflection; a time to think about the past months, but also about the deeper past, a place I find mysterious and fascinating, not least because my memory is so appallingly bad. I am bewildered when reminded of times that have left no trace, and embarrassed by the apparently perfect recall of others. What was the point in going wherever it was and doing whatever I did if the whole experience leaves no trace? Often, I feel robbed of my own history.

No wonder, then, that I have always been fascinated by how memory works, why it so often gilds the past, especially given how things generally turn out in the end, and why some people have perfect recall where others, like me, do not. Naturally enough, being with Mum is reviving my interest. Dementia is a condition that can be misconceived, to my mind at least. Seen from the outside, it appears to rob us of our faculties, memory especially; to diminish us and undermine our relationship with reality. All true, I'm sure, and depending on the individual and the symptoms of their particular form of dementia, the experience can be awful. So let me be clear, I do not pretend to speak for anyone but myself and my mum. We are fortunate. I saw the second of Mum's brothers go through Alzheimer's. I saw his bewilderment and fear, and his anger. I could only wonder at my aunt's capacity to cope, which she did valiantly over many years, without paid carers and with only her two children for support. Now that is love and care.

It so happens that my mother's dementia does not appear to cause her to be angry or frustrated, though I have to be cautious in making any assumptions from the outside. She has hallucinations that are generally benign, and I'm told this is common with Parkinson's dementia in particular. She does get down from time to time, but depression, which she certainly did suffer from in the care home, is much less of a problem now we're home and in more familiar surroundings, with people she can recognize.

When I try to give her a drink or something to eat, and all her attention is on the soldier in the room or the dogs that need feeding, I have the powerful sense that her reality, far from being diminished, is actually augmented. Her thoughts and imaginings are clearly more real than the sticky cake or the cooling coffee held in my aching hand. And in trying to get her attention, I often feel like I'm interrupting a film she's watching, or intruding on a dream. If I pay full attention to the mumbled snippets she uses to describe what she sees, almost to me, almost to herself, I can even place some of what she's experiencing in the context of her life. She's maybe imagining things, as we might see it, but she's also remembering. All those sights and sounds are coming from somewhere, and what is imagination if not the mind playing wild and free with memory?

Unlike Proust and his madeleine cake, Mum is not transported to another time and place in search of anything, or at least not for very long. Once the taste buds do their thing, the children in the garden often fade away, especially if the cake is chocolate or coffee and walnut. And yes, I'm aware of the danger of using cake to dispel illusion, to bring her back to reality, or indeed to make my own life easier. But my motive is not control or an easy life. Instead, the pure sensual joy of eating is a high not just for her, but for me too. To give such pleasure is hard to resist, and harder still for her, it seems.

I use music for the same reason. The carers were only confirmed in their notion that I was 'one to watch' when they would arrive to find Frank Sinatra or *The Best Sixties Album in the World ... Ever!* or Stan Getz or *Country Love Songs* playing as I was giving Mum breakfast or supper. I have eased most of them into the notion that there is no reason the music should be turned off in order to change Mum's pad, and every reason why music lifts the spirits and makes the task in hand just a little less onerous.

It's a trick I first used as a single dad. I had to learn
the whole plethora of skills necessary to get the girls to
school on time and with all they needed for the day.
With lunch boxes, homework, sports kit and even
musical instruments to remember, I was going down
unless I came up with something. My solution was that
they would find their own stuff and pack their own
bags and dress themselves appropriately for school. In
return, I made the solemn promise that their lunch boxes
would contain enviable sandwiches, prepared with love
and bound to impress friends, together with snack bars
from the supermarket in shiny wrapping, or packets
of high-calorie, high-salt crisps. Together we set the
whole morning routine to music, played loud enough
that I couldn't hear questions beginning with 'Where's
my …' even if I were listening. We played anything the
girls liked, from Beyoncé to Dido, and anything I liked
too, from my old stalwarts, Dean Martin singing 'That's
Amore' and Frank's take on Cole Porter's 'That's Life',
to hits of the sixties, and even *Così Fan Tutte*, though
singalongs always worked best.

Now I am with Mum, music seems to me to be
an entirely natural element in the daily landscape of
routines and chores and the long hours of simply sitting.
Together we'll listen to the same music I once played
with my children, choosing artists I first heard on my
parents' record player, or sung by my father. Mum will

often recognize one of the songs. Music is another way of connecting, accessing memory and shared experience, and if that means I become Frank Sinatra, albeit briefly, I'll take on the role with gusto.

'Ol' blue eyes is back,' I say. 'Any requests? How about "Fly Me to the Moon" or "What Is This Thing Called Love?".'

Sometimes I get nothing in return. Sometimes she says, 'Come on, hurry up.' But often she smiles – or even giggles – and then I sing all the louder. Once or twice, she has called me by my father's name. I like that music helps to bring Dad into the conversation. It feels right to acknowledge him, and her love for him, as part of our being together.

The current wisdom in dealing with dementia is never to contradict the sufferer. But just listen to the language in that statement. 'Dealing', 'contradict' and 'sufferer' are extraordinary terms to use, implying a problem to be solved and a person to be pitied. It never occurs to me to deny the visitors she sees in the garden. When she asks me who they are, I tell her I'm on it and I'll let her know. Some will say my approach is patronizing, even as others approve, but either way the plain truth is I'm rather envious of her augmented reality, and joining in with her pleases me and seems to do no harm. It seems to me she has found a way to beat being stuck in a wheelchair. She takes a trip without the help of stimulants other than that rather inventive and wonderful concoction of chemicals and electricity we call the brain. It may seem I'm romanticizing things, but I often wish I could do the same. Reality is overrated, and the fact that she's 'making things up' is, to me, more a source of wonder than worry.

Sometimes she sees a child or children I can't place precisely in her experience. Of course, they could be my sister and me, but I don't think so. Usually she talks about 'the little girl', sometimes in 'the pretty dress', and I get the sense that this girl is ethereal and unworldly, more spirit than flesh, more an ideal than a representation of the real. I talked about these hallucinations with Sylvia, the Parkinson's nurse. She told me that visions of children and dogs, or rather puppies, are very common with the disease.

Take the soldier and the dogs, for example. At the house in which Mum was brought up, on the very edge of the surrounding desert, there were a number of dogs, presumably kept for security, that lived outside. As for the soldiers, she was born in 1934 and would have been five years old at the start of the Second World War, nine or ten when it ended. I know from Uncle Pete's tales of their youth that they often had British soldiers billeted with them as they returned from the front line in the desert or waited their turn to go out.

If I can connect her hallucinations with what I know of her life experience, and if she's not too tired and I'm not too hidebound by my own one-dimensional attitude to the real, we can develop impressions and fleeting images into something more coherent, something like a narrative that in turn delivers comfort and joy. For me, anyway, and I think for us both.

These times are rare. More often, as far as I can tell, her thoughts – far from being tethered to the past – are a rich mix of imagination and the world around her, creating a very layered reality, so much more complex than mine, and somehow more real and less conscious at the same time. Often she puts me in mind of a wild animal, tame and trusting enough to allow me to feed her, but all instinct, pure and even beautiful.

I am tempted to say that it feels to me sometimes that in fact Mum lives in a kind of eternal present, which might seem to make her a prisoner of the moment, and so to our minds diminished in some way. And yet I envy her that unfettered interaction with the world. Most of us fritter our lives away with plans for the future and regrets over the past, undermining the whole notion of living in the present that is central to so many enlightened philosophies.

Zen, for instance, counsels us to live in the moment, to give up personal ambition, self-serving desires and all but the most fundamental requirements of bodily survival as a route to enlightenment and a peaceful soul. At least as far as I understand the tenets. And while there may be profound spiritual compensations, you have to be pretty hardcore to go the whole way. I am not hardcore. Or not hardcore enough. I like frivolity, fun and even excess, though in moderation, naturally. Mum, you could argue, has got a bit of Zen going on.

That is not to say dementia is a good thing. On bad days, she is disturbed by the interference of one signal with another. Certainly to me, looking in from the outside. No matter how she twists the dial, she can't tune in to reality without the intrusion of another signal altogether. And if you've ever tried to get an AM radio station with an analogue dial, or to hear a soft-spoken friend in a crowded bar, you'll know how she feels. I have bad days too; days when the hallucinations are a pain in the ass and I just want her to drink the coffee and eat the cake so I can take a break before thinking about what's for lunch.

But the bad days are rare, and usually sleep, or the lack of it, is to blame. More often, now we are alone together in a comfortable bungalow with plenty of cake and plenty of time on our hands, I realize there's a chance to reflect, to recall shared experiences, to look at old photos together, to find things in drawers that I remember from childhood, and for both of us to be reminded of what was forgotten.

My own forgetfulness is the subject of speculation among family and friends, who cannot quite decide if

I am damaged in some way, or merely pretending to forget as a convenient way to live without baggage. This, as Michel de Montaigne – humanist, essayist, philosopher and bold explorer of himself – might say, is to impugn my character without good reason. I am not faking it, any more than he was back in the sixteenth century. This is from the beginning of his essay 'Of Liars':

> There is not a man living whom it would so little become to speak from memory as myself, for I have scarcely any at all, and do not think that the world has another so marvellously treacherous as mine. My other faculties are all sufficiently ordinary and mean; but in this I think myself very rare and singular, and deserving to be thought famous.

I feel the same way, and as a consequence, I try to find ways to preserve the past. A long time ago, I made myself a box. It had a hinged lid and stood about the height of a chair seat. It was wide enough and strong enough to sit on, being made of half-inch-thick wood. My ex-wife painted the box in bright colours with a geometric pattern of her own design. I'm not sure why. Inside, I kept … stuff, aide-memoires, you might say, anything from photographs and letters to theatre tickets and hotel reservations. It was only a few months ago that my ex brought the contents to me here at the bungalow in a couple of plastic bags. She kept the box.

I've had a quick look inside the bags, and I'm thinking I might allow myself an hour or two of sustained nostalgia this very evening, after the care call, when Mum is sleeping and I'm alone. I am intrigued, but I have to say my first impression is of old tat, desiccated spiders, faded photos and orphaned bits of paper. I can remember certain items, my grandfather's cigarette-rolling machine, for instance, but I can't attach much meaning to it other than the fact that it once belonged to him. There might be more in the letters, but I have the feeling I'll be reading about someone who is a stranger to me now, with no record of what I may have written in return, and thus only a half-remembered past. I'm sure my own letters are unlikely to be preserved in anyone else's box of memories, though I suppose one never knows.

I lost half a day and a whole night dusting off photographs and reading letters, paying calls on people and places I have not visited in a very long time, unable even to focus on the care call, going to bed only to dream confused and concocted scenes animated by all I had found.

What I did not find was bundles of correspondence from my mother to me. I found only one letter, in fact, airmail and written to me at university two years after she, along with my father and sister, had emigrated to Washington, DC. I would have been twenty years old. She spoke of her hopes that my exams had gone well and that I was not short of money, and she gave me a rundown on the bearings in her car's steering that had been faulty and were now repaired. My family lived in America for more than ten years, but that is the only letter from my mother that has survived. There were many more, I'm sure, but I did not keep them, either because I am a careless son or because they did not seem worth keeping. My father did not write.

I thought I might find something she had written when I was a young boy or a teenager. When I was thirteen or so, I spent a year at a boarding school; not the posh sort, but a shape-up-and-stand-tall kind of place run by a former military man along military lines, designed to take children who were not thriving in the state system and give them a chance to flourish in the countryside. I have letters from my grandmother from that time, but none from my mother, though again, I'm sure she would have written to me. I am both surprised and disappointed.

I have an even sadder admission following my fruitless search through the bags of tat. If I am forced to rely solely on my memory to uncover my relationship with my mother, I can muster nothing more than five or ten fleeting impressions; mere snapshots of insignificant moments that do absolutely nothing to tell her story or reveal her character.

The only way I can find to source anything at all is by squinting my eyes and conjuring a place rather than her. For example, if I picture the house we lived in until I was eleven or twelve, I can recall the magnolia in the front garden and the feel of the spongy petals I would squeeze between finger and thumb. I can see the brick of the outside walls and the leaded lights of the bay window to the right; I can feel the weight of the front door, made of wood and studded with iron decoration in imitation of something far grander and older. If I concentrate, I can walk through the hallway, past the stairs and the door to the front room, past the coat cupboard where I would hide when it came time for school, burying myself under a mountain of shoes, to where I can just see my mother in the kitchen cooking. If I lose focus for even a moment, she is still there, but the kitchen has shifted to the next house we lived in, when I was a teenager. I remember particularly a pressure cooker that fascinated me. It always whistled like a high-pitched steam train. I can hear my mother telling me not to keep touching the valve for fear I would scald myself. I'm asking her questions that in my imagination are to do with food – what I am allowed, what is for supper and whether there are any Frosties – and I can vaguely hear her saying that I should not use all the milk.

I am back in the old house. I see the bay window of the L-shaped bedroom with its broad sill, broad enough for me to sit on and read, or play with tiny Afrika Korps plastic soldiers, bayonets drawn, or reeling backwards, arms akimbo, moments after being shot by the enemy, knocking them over as the battle progressed till none were left standing. On the dining room table there is a bloody piece of paper that holds a whole and surprisingly large cow's eye. I am cutting into the eye with a scalpel, trying to remove the lens and the jelly and then to scrape at the retina to make up a slide I can examine under my microscope.

My mother is in my sister's bedroom. I am there too, because my own bedroom has a tight turn I cannot negotiate on crutches. I have broken my leg, a spiral fracture of the tibia, caused by the bone snapping over the top of my ski boot when I fell and the bindings failed to release. I have a long plaster from ankle to hip, cut open down the front in order to allow the soft tissues to swell without undue pain. My mother has brought me a washing-up bowl of warm soapy water because I cannot have a bath, and I am telling her that I can wash myself because I am fourteen and I don't want her to wash me.

Then, because memory has no respect for chronology and delivers fleeting images in random order, I see myself as seven years old, or even younger, five perhaps. The curtains are closed, it is night and my mother is getting ready to go out. The only light is from the mirrored bedside table, built into the headboard. There is the red silky bedspread I remember so well, with the floral pattern in the same colour. I can feel the silk under my fingertips. I remember how the bedspread slips and slides, so if you pull too hard it might all come slithering towards you and fall to the floor. I am watching her put on a dress. I am tucked under the blankets. Maybe I have been allowed to sleep there until she and my father return from their night out. I think her hair and make-up are done, and she has the scent of perfume about her. She is rushing, trying to put on a girdle and garter belt, I can't be sure, mysterious armour-plating to my childish mind, and besides, she has her back to me. Having retrieved that image, my mind allows me a glimpse of a goodnight kiss, maybe later the same night when they have returned from their 'do'. Now I can smell cigarette smoke on my mother and I can hear my father's voice, louder because he is drunk, and I can feel my hand in hers as she leads me from their bed to my own, sleepy and grumpy at being displaced.

If I were to squint long enough, I might be able to recover more of these disconnected memories, though I doubt they will reveal much. Is this my failing only? Did I simply not pay attention to my mother?

Or perhaps it is a boy thing. We boys tend to see our mothers as providers, mainly of food, but of other things too, like validation and unconditional love. We can see those gifts as a one-way street, from her to me, from them to us. All children are selfish, that's how they survive. But ask any boy, 'What's your mother's favourite colour? What food does she love? What makes her heart sing?' and I wonder how many could guess and even come close. Would a girl know her father's favourite food? Almost certainly.

Or maybe this forgetting is common to us all; certainly I read somewhere that the curse of a poor memory is simple survival. Were we to remember too much, we might drown in the past. So in order to live in the present, we overlay our memories, particularly where people are concerned. Recent incarnations erase older versions of ourselves and our loved ones. Maybe my mother as she was then no longer exists, overlaid by my mother as she is here and now.

The fleeting images and impressions lingering in my mind of a whistling pressure cooker or a red silk bedspread are little better than a plastic bag of dusty old photographs and letters. I can hardly lay claim to any kind of meaningful narrative of my own life, let alone hers.

★

It is five o'clock in the evening. The news is just starting on Radio 4 and I am preparing a sundowner for us both in the kitchen, now an established ritual before I prepare supper and one of the carers arrives for the evening care call. I can see Mum through the window. She is sitting in her wheelchair in the garden, where I left her only a few minutes ago with the promise of a gin and tonic and some cheesy snacks to come. I stop what I'm doing for a moment, no longer hearing the voice on the radio telling me of events in the outside world, just to wonder at the strange good fortune of our ending up here in this place together. A sense of deep satisfaction comes over me.

Mum is wide awake when I put our drinks on the hospital table in front of her. She looks surprised to see me, and not altogether certain who I am. When I sit and then lean in close, she says the dogs are out and need feeding. I offer up the gin and tonic. She takes a sip and glances quickly to her left, as if something or someone has caught her attention. I ask her what she sees. She tells me the little girl needs to go home. I tell her I'll see to it right after we've had our drink. Reassured, her lips purse, ready for another sip and her fingers pinch at my hand as if to help me hold the glass.

Mum was prescribed pills to reduce the tremor she doesn't have, an anti-emetic to combat the side effects of the tremor meds, and another pill to counteract her low blood pressure and so prevent falls that can't happen anyway because she can't stand up to walk – and that's not because of the gin, by the way. But Sylvia, our specialist Parkinson's nurse, who visits every couple of months, has written to the GP on our behalf, and the number of pills each day has been reduced from sixteen to four. She has also approved the sundowner, always assuming moderation reigns.

It feels colder now I am outside with Mum, and I wonder if we should still be in the garden at this time of year, even though the sun is still warm and an Indian summer is in full swing. So maybe there are no shoulds. Or maybe, as I suspect, there's a whole rulebook I should follow, and don't; a rulebook that almost certainly bars me from bringing a sundowner to a Parkins on's dementia patient who is fragile in every conceivable way. And yet a gin and tonic and an afternoon in the garden as the air cools is precisely the kind of risk I like to encourage. The kind of risk that makes you pretty certain you're alive; the kind that relieves the aches and pains and makes you aware only of the sun on your face, and the warmth of the breeze, and the piquancy of a summer that is almost done.

Perhaps I'm projecting. How can I be sure my mother doesn't want to be indoors, where it's warmer? Perhaps a gin and tonic with ice and lemon is no match for a cup of tea she can try her best to suck up through a straw from a plastic cup with wing handles. It is true to say that I cannot be sure. I have no proof. I could ask her, but binary questions – 'Would you like this, or this?' – seem in my experience to set up a conflict in her mind that leaves her at a loss, and all questions are hard to compute when your inner life is as rich as hers, with dogs to be fed and little girls to send home. So I have to guess. I have to take a chance on what works, and live with the consequences if it doesn't. I choose to do so based solely on this notion: what would I want if I were her?

Putting yourself in someone else's shoes may not qualify as a principle, but as a strategy, it has one important merit. The application of experience and imagination, together with intuition – as opposed to the one-size-fits-all guidance of a rulebook – can, with someone you've known all your life, and loved too, mean you end up sharing a simple moment of pleasure and reflection like this one.

XXII

There was a frost this morning. The first of the year. I looked out of the kitchen window, beyond the rescued orchid that sits on the sill, to see the grass of the back garden lightly dusted in silver, with fox prints in pale green. A frost is not unusual for the third week of October, but it is a reminder of the impending winter. I fear the days to come will drag horribly, though I try not to look too far ahead and to keep my focus on the here and now.

Take today. It could have been a rough one, but in the end it turned out fine because I am learning what to expect, and even what to do. The urinary tract infection that landed Mum in hospital only a little while ago has twice since tried its hand, and twice been repelled, though I am still crossing my fingers with this latest incarnation, which flared up only yesterday afternoon. The signs that we might need outside help are still hard to distinguish from the normal ups and downs of Mum's weak immune system and her remarkable ability to self-heal given the right conditions. Smelly brown urine and heightened confusion are still the most reliable signs, but in both cases it is a question of degree. My response – and that of the carers – is to keep watching, to be slow to escalate but quick to react when the red line we set for ourselves is reached. This is usually a consensus, and often a question of time. If, over a certain period, symptoms do not recede with paracetamol, rehydration sachets, plenty of fluids, including cranberry juice, and live yoghurt, then an antibiotic is the only option, always carrying with it the risk that a prescribing doctor could also precipitate a hospital stay if sepsis or some other complication is suspected.

Doctors must err on the side of caution, just as hospitals must, and because Mum is so vulnerable, home visits are the order of the day, all of which means it is impossible to know which doctor will appear at the door and whether he or she will know Mum as anything more than a printout of her recent medical history, studied on arrival. The last time her symptoms required an antibiotic, the doctor asked if I could collect a urine sample from Mum before his house call. The idea came as news to me. He said I could pick up a tube and label from the surgery and then send it to the lab for analysis, where they would determine the precise bug we were dealing with.

So when yesterday Mum's skin was flushed – though I could find no fever – and the morning pad had been 'offensive', in the jargon of the carers, I asked at the surgery for a sample kit, and when Lisa arrived for the care call this morning, we sat Mum on the commode, wrapped in towels to keep her warm, and waited.

If getting a sample kit is straightforward, getting a sample is often much trickier, but we were lucky, and after half an hour, I had just enough to fill a third of the sample tube.

'All right?' Lisa asked as she wheeled Mum from the bathroom to the bedroom.

'Yeah, I think so. There should be just enough.'

'Well done, and good news on number twos … got a result, so no need to worry about that.'

It's astonishing how comfortable I've become with sharing such intimate information, but it is vital to know that Mum's body is doing what it should. Being aware of what comes out has become as natural to me as making sure she is eating and drinking enough.

I'm not claiming any credit, except perhaps for knowing a little more about how things work, for pushing the system, even if it pushed back, and for becoming a better advocate. Small changes perhaps, but enough to make a genuine difference to my mother's well-being and survival.

I'm learning other lessons too. I have begun to realize that in order to care well, you have to worry less. You can't fix everything. Some days are good, some not so good; sometimes you can laugh together and sometimes it is all too much and what you want to do is weep. In worrying about what is to come, I achieve absolutely nothing. It is about having less investment in outcomes and bearing less responsibility for what happens, while at the same time being more expert and better able to judge situations and assert Mum's best interests as I see them. I know there is a distinction between what I can do and what I can't do, what I can fix and what I can't fix. I know, too, that not everything that goes wrong is my fault. Sometimes I screw up, but a lot of the time I don't, and when I do, I learn to do things differently in the future.

When care is the exclusive concern of an outside agency, when it is confined to an institution and hidden from view to the rest of us, when it falls on the shoulders of one family member, who is expected to dedicate their own life to that of another, it becomes a burden and a problem for society. When care is shared and carers are supported, trained, rewarded and valued, it becomes love extended to the end of life.

Our lives are circular. We begin our existence on

the planet in the care of others and we will likely end it in the same way. We are making the same journey from cradle to grave, from being cared for to caring for, from giving to receiving, ebbing and flowing throughout.

I was feeling pretty smug as I cleaned my teeth and got ready for bed. Mum had taken the first two doses of the antibiotic I'd picked up from the chemist this afternoon, and I was running through my achievements in negotiating the system and avoiding escalation. I'd squeezed the pad, filled the tube, neatly sidestepped the wrath and rules of the surgery receptionists – a fearsome lot, defensive of their brood of young doctors. I had made a modest proposal to the prescribing doctor with regard to the most effective antibiotic, and my mother was now sleeping peacefully in her own bed.

Genie and I are still writing. Sometimes I sit with the laptop in bed and look for an email from her before I go to sleep. Even though she is still slow to reply, I find I'm beginning to rely on our correspondence as a kind of consolation at the end of a long day. When she does write, the banter is good and we're slowly getting to know each other. I can tease her now, as I did recently when I had a terrible toothache and she took her time responding to my plight.

Dear Dr Genie,

It is with deep regret that I must inform you of the passing of the patient due to heart complications beyond our control.

One anecdote. When I was passing one day on my rounds, I heard him call to me. I sat beside him on the bed, though it's strictly against regulations. I suppose I had a sense this might be our last conversation. 'Doc,' he said, sounding like a bad American movie, 'we both know, don't we? It's the end.'

He lay back on the bed, eyes glazed, and his lips began to form the word 'Doc' once again, so I clamped my hand over his mouth and tweaked the tube leading from the drip. That seemed to revive him.

'It's okay,' he said in a muffled voice. 'It's like floating when you get close.' At least, I think that's what he said. I still had my hand over his mouth. 'Tell Genie I ...'

Those were his last words.

We will always be grateful to you, Doctor, as I know you were inclined to take a personal interest in this man's case until your commitments at Mud Island prevented further consultation.

With all best wishes,
Dr Gum de Sease

Genie took to her role as a consultant and wrote back in kind. I was still rereading her witty words and laughing when the phone rang.

A call at ten thirty at night could only be bad, and yet everything in my world was fine. It was my ex-wife at the other end.

'It's Maisie,' she said. 'She's really bad tonight. I think it's time.'

XXIII

Do dogs know they are going to die?

Maisie had been bad for a long time, though none of us – including her – wanted to acknowledge just how bad. In the two months since I'd last seen my ex, she had given me regular updates that were far from hopeful. Maisie's legs would give out on her without warning. Her balance was shot to pieces and she had a hacking cough that was steadily getting worse. She was in pain. She could no longer run or jump and she sometimes gave a little yelp when she was lifted onto the back seat of the car. And she slept a lot. She'd had medication from the vet, but no clear diagnosis bar arthritis and the kind of lung trouble associated with advancing years. Insulated from the day-to-day reality by our physical separation in recent times, I'd felt pangs of sorrow and pity, but avoided the glaring implication that a springer spaniel of thirteen – ninety-one in human years, or so we're told – was experiencing not a temporary setback in her health, but the inevitable downward slide towards death. Just like Mum, just like me, just like us all, but rather more imminently.

My ex called again early this morning, before seven, to say she had been up all night and planned to call the vet as soon as the office was open. She had already checked out the possibility of his coming to the house to administer the injection, and she was hoping he or one of his colleagues would come today, even though it was a Saturday. She told me it had to be right away, for all our sakes. Things had got so bad overnight that all they could do was sit with Maisie, rub painkillers on her gums and hold her.

I said I would be there as soon as I could. My ex asked how I would manage with the care, and I said I would find a way. I thought of Ellie, but I might be away for some hours and the responsibility was enormous for someone with no experience at all. It had to be one of the carers. Lisa was scheduled to come this morning, in just a couple of minutes. Which meant Claire was likely to be on her day off. I knew she had dogs. Maybe she could give me cover. It was worth a try, and I'd pay cash.

Claire picked up the phone and I explained the situation and offered her fifty pounds for the morning, another fifty if I was late coming back. 'I don't want paying,' she said, 'but I can't get there until ten because

I'm halfway through doing the horses and there's no one else here.'

I thanked her, and said I'd wait. Then the phone rang again. It was my ex. The vet was booked for eleven o'clock. It was eight thirty and we still had to shower Mum, but there was just time to make it.

I feel almost nothing as I begin the hour-and-a-half drive to my old home, except the utter strangeness of making a journey so far away from my new home. The day is bright and cold, the blue of the sky pale like water covered by thin ice.

Ten miles into the trip, and I'm in virgin territory, unnerved by the big skies and the three-lane motorways and the sheer speed of the cars overtaking me. I have become institutionalized, not having travelled far in my time as a carer because I cannot leave my charge. There is a sense of exhilaration along with the fear, like a prisoner released, and something about the newness is shielding me from any feeling of grief, as if the unreality of the trip has made Maisie's fate unreal too. I wonder if this isn't a good thing. My role is not to show up and break down, but to try to be the one my daughters and ex-wife can lean on, the one who has not been up for several nights watching our dog die by degrees. I have been absent from the day-to-day. I am an outsider here now, so maybe I can use the objectivity that brings to hold it together.

I want to be strong. I want to be calm and wise. I want to do this well. As I begin to pass the familiar landmarks of schools and shops and pubs that were once part of my daily life, I look left and right to see what's changed, to see if there is anyone I recognize. As I head up our lane, passing the park and the swings where the girls played and where I taught them to cycle, I think I am going to do okay. We'll see.

My old home is a plain end-of-terrace house on a dirt track that skirts the town's cemetery before heading into the woods that extend away from the town and towards the higher ground of the South Downs. The terrace was once an early hospital – known as a 'pestilence house' – for those with infectious diseases, hence its isolated situation conveniently close to the graveyard. It became houses sometime in the nineteenth century. Our house was last occupied by three sisters who never married, lived into their eighties and died within a month of each other, one just before Christmas, the second on Boxing Day and the last in the cold depths of mid-January, as if their lives were so intertwined they could not survive one without the other. I know this because all three are buried in the family plot just beyond the garden's end.

For us, a young couple with young children, this place was a haven and a wonderland. It still is for my ex-wife and my daughters. I always have to take a breath as I make my way down the dirt path, because coming here affects me deeply. I am alone in the garden that surrounds the house on three sides. The cottage nestles low in the ground with steps down to the front door under a tile-hung porch. There is a brick-built 'bothy', an outside kitchen separate from the house, half its height buried below the ground for insulation, the ancient chimney losing its mortar and cracked from top to bottom. I remember how, once we had cleared the brambles from around the front door and fought our way into the long-deserted house, we spent the first few months painting and decorating, brushing cream and orange and Mediterranean blue over the stark white and brown of another era. We never quite got around to the outside of the house. The garden is my ex-wife's canvas, her great love in life, and I look around to see what changes she has made since last I was here: a holly tree, a stone edging relaid, *objets d'art* carefully sited among the beds of long grasses. Then I see, with a start – only a few feet away, where the paths cross – the mound of earth and the shallow grave.

It's time. Soon the vet will be here, and I have a part to play. I take the steps two at a time and glimpse my family through the window, gathered together around the sofa. I reach the green front door, the paint flaking and scuffed, pushing and lifting with elbow and foot in one practised, remembered move. I feel like an intruder in a home that is familiar and foreign. My family is waiting for me, tear-streaked, exhausted and pleading for comfort I can't provide.

Maisie is lying among them on the sofa, her head propped on a cushion and her eyes half closed. She sees me and her tail slaps against the sofa, intermittently, weakly, but just like it always does and always has. As I kneel down with my face close to hers, I can feel her breath on my skin as she tries to lift her head. She does, just a little, just enough that I can slip my hand beneath and feel the weight of her as she relaxes.

She has always liked me to scratch the inside flap of her long ears. Now I am gentle, reverent in a silly way, and her breathing is so soft it scares me. Time vanishes utterly as we fuss her with pillows and blankets and see her wince at the pain, and offer sips of water as she tries and fails to cough. We talk in quiet voices to each other and tell the beginning of stories we all know, of times gone by, of a puppy in a box, or at the beach learning to swim in our arms, of pheasants chased and chocolate cakes demolished, of ordinary times, of Cornwall and the camper van. Of it all.

And then, far too soon, the vet is here. Maisie is lifting her head, not sure of who this is, looking for guidance, nervous to find this man sitting close. He is talking softly like us, paying attention, efficient, reaching into his black doctor's bag, big and square and hard and open on the ground beside him. And there it is, the syringe, first in one hand and then the other, made nearly invisible, like a conjuror. A vial is upside down. Liquid. And now all I can see is Maisie. She is looking straight into my eyes and asking me, 'Is this all right?'

I don't hesitate. I don't waver. I tell her it *is* all right. I take my eyes from hers for the merest moment, so the vet knows I have said yes. I keep telling her it's all right as her eyes begin to close. I tell her it is all right until he lays her head down and she lies still, still here, but not here. We thank him, then he leaves and we all sit with her for the longest time, telling even quieter stories now, with fewer words, with hugs and strokes and all of us cherishing the warmth of her, still there for us to touch.

It was only after an hour, even two, that we finally wrapped Maisie in a blanket and I gathered her up in my arms to take her out into the garden. The cold air hit me and made me shiver. I laid her in the hard earth and we all moved slowly around her in a daze, and because I had to go back to be with Mum, I did not help to cover her over and hide her from the light.

I don't remember leaving, or the journey back to the bungalow. I have only the vaguest recollection of Claire's shrugs and 'What can you do?' as I gave her a fifty-pound note, and another thirty, she protesting and both of us a little embarrassed. When she was gone, I sat for a while with Mum. She was in bed, already fed and watered. Claire and I had changed her pad before she left. There was nothing to do but sit. I thought I might tell her about what had happened. But I wondered if I should. Perhaps Maisie's story would call to mind other dogs from other times and places, our old Labrador, for instance. That might not be a good thing before falling asleep. So I kissed her on the forehead and said we would talk in the morning. I pressed the electric button to lower the bed, tugged at the slide sheet to put her on her side, propping her back with a pillow, another between her knees and another under her knees, and only when I reached the door did I realize how much I would have liked to talk with her.

The weak light spilling from the kitchen window falls on the garden. There is no moon, and though I can hear the trees rushing this way and that in the wind, I cannot see them, black against a black sky. It's cold. I have a coat on and I am holding a wine glass by its rim, low to one side of my body. I wonder why I have yet to cry. It's not as if I don't cry easily – my younger daughter singing, or seeing my elder skip with happiness, just as she used to as a five-year-old, can melt me to mush. Perhaps there is no point in crying if you're alone, as I am tonight.

Seeing my books still lining the shelves at the old house, kneeling on the rug we bought on our travels in India, long before children, knowing the MG Sprite we drove through France on our honeymoon was sitting covered in dust in the garage, bearing the surprising weight of Maisie's body in my arms, none of this tipped me into tears. I had promised myself I would be strong for my daughters and my ex-wife who had borne so much of the lead-up to today, but it's not that either. So what is it?

How have I become so remote from myself?

XXIV

I have a doctor's appointment today. For me, nothing to do with Mum, and not because of any embarrassing complaint. The skin tags are history now, though I have the kit with the elastic bands under the bathroom sink in case of a recurrence.

Dr Brody is only a few years older than my daughters. 'Hello again,' she says as I close the door to her room. Her familiarity makes me realize I have seen doctors, usually her, more often this year than ever before in my life. It's all been minor stuff, like the ankle that twanged one morning six months ago as I got out of bed and then persisted through physio and beyond. Or the chest infection caused by smoking and always hitting me hard in the winter. I have cut down and I will give up.

I hand her the leaflet the kind lady from carers' support gave me before Mum came home. It details a government scheme that offers full-time carers a single one-off payment of five hundred pounds in their first year of caring. The idea is that you spend the money on your own well-being by joining a gym, or getting a counsellor, or, I suppose, a beauty treatment, if that's what makes you feel good. I can't see any restrictions on how the money should be used, bar the fact that a doctor has to sign it off first, vouching for the fact that I am a full-time carer and that my mental health would benefit.

'Have you had any mental health issues?' Dr Brody asks.

'No,' I say, 'or yes if that means you can sign it off. Caring is hard. Harder than I thought it would be. And there are no days off.'

'Do you know how you would spend the money?'

'Not exactly,' I say, 'but I'm a thousand pounds overdrawn as I sit here, so it shouldn't be a problem. I only have my carer's allowance of sixty pounds a week.'

I know exactly what I want to do with the five hundred pounds, though I have yet to tell anyone, including the doctor, because I know it will raise eyebrows. It may even cause a storm.

The last couple of weeks since Maisie died have left me feeling dislocated. Things are shifting around me. There is slippage, and I'm hoping it doesn't signal an earthquake of some kind. Lisa is quitting care. There have been grumbles all along about the hourly rate, mileage payments and working hours, but I have got used to the complaints as pure background noise. Now she has handed in her notice, and Claire is likely to follow suit. If they go, when they go, the agency says it may cease operating in our area. All of which means I am scrabbling around for a new agency, and meeting the same objections I met when I first embarked on this.

Then there was a visit from an official of the American Embassy. He came down from London in a cab, a sixty-mile round trip, to make sure Mum was alive and was who she said she was, or more accurately, who *I* said she was. They had cut her social security payments, due from the time my parents had spent living in America, and I have been fighting a paper war ever since. Only establishing her identity face to face would constitute proof of a legitimate claim. He used words just like that on the phone. He arrived, the cab waited, and the man stood at the end of Mum's bed, looking deeply uncomfortable, and politely asked her to confirm her identity. Nothing. He asked again, but the sentence trailed off halfway through. He turned to me and said, 'I won't take up more of your time, I'm satisfied this is your mother.'

Even across the Atlantic, things are falling apart. My sister's relationship has reached the point where she has moved out and into an apartment of her own. I've emailed her to tell her about Maisie and about Mum's odd visitor, but we have yet to catch up on the phone. I hope we will talk tonight, and if we do, I will tell her about the plan I have in mind, because it relies on her holding the fort here in the lead-up to Christmas, and because even with the government's five hundred pounds, it will need a subsidy from my sister if it is to go ahead.

And there's my younger daughter. The experimental procedure that might save her from a full hip replacement has been postponed and there is no firm date for when it will be rescheduled, bar sometime in the spring. This is a blow, but there is nothing any of us can do. What she wants is for the whole business to go away. What she would settle for is that it should not define her or limit her life. She sings like an angel, with a soul sound that is pitch perfect. She writes songs too, most of them sad these days, I notice.

And then there's me. Me in myself, I mean. Because I wasn't altogether truthful with the doctor on that score either. Something is wrong, but I don't know what. I feel numb and remote from it all. I look at Mum, who is thriving on a diet of cake and care and is blissfully ignorant of climate change, Middle Eastern wars and migrants drowning in the oceans. Nor does she really know how I feel. I don't blame her; how could I? But neither do I feel what I should in the way of compassion. I'm all compassioned out.

Not only is crying beyond me, the laughter has vanished too. I do not want to accept that this is the beginning of the end for me, and yet all I can see ahead is a whole lot more of the same. Like Mum, I could go on for years, but is that a good thing? Is that what I want? To eat cake and defecate until an organ stops doing what it should, or a rogue cell breeds thousands of deformed cells in its own image and decides it is my time to go?

I'm not depressed, not yet, but I can see it coming. I know because I've felt like this before; only once, but I believe that if you've opened up those neural pathways in your mind, you can always take an unexpected detour. Last time, I ran away. I don't want to do that again – I can't – but neither can I bear feeling so trapped and airless. Which is why I have made a plan to cauterize all this before I begin to wallow in my own horseshit.

My sister has been telling me to take a break. She says I'm stressed. She says she can hear it in my voice, and that when she comes for Christmas, I should think about taking a couple of nights in the New Forest to grab a little 'me' time. I *am* stressed, and a bit stuck, and very disappointed in myself. Where's the Zen now? Where's the sense of humour? Where is the old me? I want those things back, which is maybe why I've come up with a variation on the theme of a short break …

Two nights in Havana, two nights at the Varadero beach resort, full board no less, and three days between to catch a bus all the way across the island of Cuba. My goal is to reach the Escambray Mountains and walk the same trails as William Morgan, the hero of the book I was writing in France and have not touched since becoming a carer. I get to do that for seven hundred and ninety-nine pounds all in, including transfers. A last-minute deal, normally over a thousand, but I have got to be quick if I want to do it. With the government's five hundred pounds and the two hundred pounds I still have from the money Uncle Pete gave me all those months ago, I only need a hundred from my sister, maybe two with spending money. She will want to give me the cash, but I will insist on a loan. And I will pay her back when I can work again, or perhaps when the book finally sells.

I don't deserve such indulgence. Of course I don't. There are thousands, even millions of carers out there who care night and day for years and get no reward like the one I'm planning. I have been a carer for only eight months, and if I have yet to have a day off, that could be arranged without flying to the Caribbean. There are carers who care for loved ones who no longer recognize them, or worse, resent the care and the carer, kicking against their fate. And here am I with a mother who, on at least two occasions since we've been here together, has said to me, 'You're wonderful.'

But I don't feel wonderful.

'I think you should do it,' my sister says when we talk on the phone. 'It's not just the caring; it's been a tough year, starting with Dad.'

'I am Dad.'

'No you're not.'

'We have the same address. We live with the same woman. I get letters addressed to him.'

She is quiet at the other end. My sister doesn't like it when I sound crazy. She worries about me. She thinks what I'm doing is worthy of huge respect, but it pains her when I sound strung out. I'm sitting at Dad's old desk while we speak and scrolling through emails on my computer when I see I have a new message from Genie.

'I know how hard it was for you with Dad, especially in the last ten years, but maybe, I mean … You haven't really grieved at all, you know?'

I'm reading and listening at the same time. Genie's daughter is learning to drive. Genie is teaching her before she goes …

'For Dad?' I say.

'Why not? He was our father, it's normal to feel something.'

'Like relief? Like a chance to finally be with Mum? Too little too late, but he did the right thing in the end.'

Africa. I read the word again. Genie is moving there. Permanently.

'And look, I know it's not the same, but even with

Maisie, you haven't said much of anything, and I know how much she mattered to you … I'm just worried about you, that's all.'

It starts then. I feel my throat tighten. I try to swallow and I can't, but I know that if I don't, the tears are going to come. So I take a breath, but it catches, and my sister hears.

'Are you okay?'

I don't answer, because I can't. I don't know if it's Genie, or Maisie, or Dad, or Mum, or me, or what, but I can't stop it.

'What is it? Is it what I said about Dad?'

I want to answer, but when I try, it ends in a spluttering cough.

'Speak to me?'

'Hang on,' I say.

I go to the bathroom and pull sheets of toilet paper from the roll to clear the snot. I take some back to the phone just in case.

'I'm back,' I say. 'Bound to happen.'

'Tell me you're okay.'

'I'm okay. I really am. I've just had a shock, that's all. Remember I told you about Genie?'

'Uh-huh. This is GreenGenie, rhino lady, right?'

'She's moving to Africa. She's going there to save rhinos.'

'Well, that makes sense. But that's a good thing, no?'

'If you're a rhino. But I guess it means she won't be saving me.'

'This is a woman you've never met.'

I make a noise that, for all I know, may well sound like a very distant rhino in distress.

'Are you laughing or crying? I can't tell.'

'Nor can I.'

There are times when you come face to face with a true reflection of yourself, unmediated, undeniable and uncomfortable though it is.

For most of our lives, we perceive ourselves through the distorting prisms of desire and regret, the one tied to the future and the other to the past. We imagine a better, happier self in the future, when this happens or that goes away, when an ambition is satisfied or a change made. We pick over the past, rerunning people and events in a loop, hoping that this time the story will hang together, that we will recognize a hinterland that makes sense of all we are and all we have become.

Of course, I understand there is no narrative to our lives. I get it that our pattern-making brains cannot help but order the chaos of existence. We can't skip forward to see what happens next, and even if we could, the universe is contingent and might well change the plot before it has played out. Nor can we change the past. We are *in medias res*, relating our stories from the middle of the action, but it seems to me that we still have to try to tell the truth, even if it is only partial.

Here is my view from the bridge. I have been too long a dreamer. I idealized Genie because of a photograph, because of a resemblance she bore to my ex-wife and to Marie, but above all because that one photograph reminded me of Audrey Hepburn, and so my mother. Mum has always been an ideal in my life. She was always there for me, but never quite there as a person in her own right, never entirely knowable, even before dementia. Her Mona Lisa smile gave nothing away, then and now. If my father's dominant personality and coercive control served to crush her as an independent person and so obscure her even further from me, I still wonder that I know so little about her. It is true to say that my uncle, too remembers her only as a sister who was there for him, but without knowing her well himself. It is also true that the times dictated that women should see themselves in terms of their ability to meet the needs of others, but that is not Mum's whole story. Perhaps that will remain hidden forever.

But if my mother is an enigma, it is only since being with her that I have come to understand that we have much in common. I am a father first and foremost, and now a carer. But I am a good father, not because I wanted to be better than him, but because of my mother, because there is so much of her in me, or at least the best of me. She taught me about the quietness of love, about its humility and patience, and if I have often been selfish, or angry, sometimes mean or overbearing, she has always been my ideal, my lodestone for how to behave.

I did not know all this before I became her carer. Because all my life, I have defined myself not by reference to her, but by trying to be as unlike my father as it is possible to be. I look at myself in his bathroom mirror, and the old man I see is both me and him. There's a crease on my forehead where I sleep with one hand under the temple and crumple my face as a result. He had the same crease in the same place, and I've no doubt it was there for the same reason. But whatever the resemblance, I know I have always thought and acted in reaction to him, rebelling against his values, his view of what matters and his view of me, his son. His craving for genteel suburbia versus my yearning to bask in bohemia. His need for security lights and deadbolts on every door versus my total lack of material possessions, a home being only the most valuable. Does it not bother you, he asked me once, to own so little? Even my being here with Mum has been a way of rebelling against him, showing him I can do what he couldn't.

No accident, then, that I would choose to spend years writing about a natural-born rebel like William Morgan, a man always kicking against authority.

'It's ancient history,' my father said when I told him I was writing about the fifties. 'Why would you do that? And why him?'

Why indeed? I see now that Morgan has been a cipher for something, perhaps for my father. Maybe that is why I can't write the book, because in a sense, our story is not finished. I could go to Cuba and I might find Morgan, or his ghost. But there is another ghost that haunts me, one that I see from time to time when I look in the mirror, a ghost I have to lay to rest if I am to become myself, perhaps for the first time in my life.

Even at this late stage, I want the man in the mirror to be me, not him.

We're told that life is loss. For me, a marriage has come and gone, Genie – who I know was never really there – is going, Marie has gone, even Maisie has gone. But it is also true that were it not for all I've lost, or squandered, along the way, I wouldn't be here, and neither would Mum. I would never have learned lessons from her in what it is to care, in endurance certainly, in letting go of the past and the future and living in the moment. And I would never have had this time to reflect.

I would have missed so many lessons in love.

WINTER

XXV

We're driving to the airport again. Only this time my sister is at the wheel and I'm the passenger. She's squinting at the glare of winter sun on wet roads and leaning forward in her seat, still getting used to driving on the left. So I hesitate before I ask her, 'Are you sure you're okay with this, Sis? You don't mind that I'm going to Ireland ... and without you?'

'I'm fine with it if you are. This is your thing.'

'Maybe this is mad. I could have been on my way to Havana.'

'True, and you're unlikely to get much of a suntan in Derry. Your choice.'

'I know. But is it the right choice?'

'You have to do this, for you. Isn't that what you said?'

'But it's Christmas Eve tomorrow, and with the family coming ...'

'Look, the prep is done. We've got the turkey, that's all that was worrying me, and there's a whole wine cellar in the garage now. Stop worrying.'

'And Phil?'

'He can have your bed tonight and the floor tomorrow. We'll raise a glass tonight. Like I said, stop worrying. Have you got everything?'

'It's just Dad and me, and a toothbrush.'

When she drops me at the terminal, I take the wheelie bag and kiss her goodbye. She looks rueful, but says nothing. I go to the desk to check in, and I'm still wondering about putting the bag in the hold, even though it's fine as carry-on. There's no customs, but there is security to think about, and I'm just not sure I want to explain what I'm taking with me, alongside a change of clothes and a wash kit. In the end, I keep the bag with me and it goes through the scanner fine.

I while away the time until the flight is called in the bookshop. Every time I fly, I browse the shelves for thrillers and adventure tales, just to see where my book would be, assuming it is ever finished. I like to check out the competition. I look for exactly the right place on the shelves, cover facing out preferably, and picture it sitting there, endorsements and all, and for a moment it all seems possible. But I don't feel inclined to buy anything, not even a newspaper. After all, the flight is only an hour and a half, and having been landlocked for so long, I can spend my time looking out the window at the Irish Sea below, and maybe treat myself to a beer or a gin and tonic.

We land in Derry to wind and rain, but then it is December. I know there's a bus that will take me up the coast towards Tullagh Strand, but nothing that will go all the way, so I've elected to splash out on a hire car for the forty-minute road trip north to the coast. I had a fantasy I might hire a taxi to take me there, but the chances of meeting a real-life Paddy Reilly seemed remote and a tad romantic. I've booked a room at the Railway Tavern in Fahan because they have traditional music and an open fire. I'll need to warm my bones after such a day, and besides, I'm a tourist in Ireland, despite my newly acquired Irish passport. I filled in the paperwork and back it came six weeks later. When I realized that Dad's heritage allowed me the privilege of being a European still, I thought, why not? Though I knew I wouldn't have to show it, I have it with me, just because I like the idea.

Derry airport is small and the hire car is waiting for me. I follow signs to the city and cross the River Foyle to head along the Donegal coast towards Muff and Quigley's Point, before cutting inland and across to Tullagh Strand, a horseshoe bay with a gorgeous beach that I picked out from the map simply because it had the word 'strand' in the name. I can picture the scene of the woman calling to her man in the story that Dad used to tell. I don't know how to find the place where he was born, or where he went to school. His birth certificate names a village near Strabane in the North, but that's not why I'm here. It's not roots I'm after. I only hope that my choice is the right one.

The countryside around me is brown heath as far as the eye can see, and there are no trees, just sky, vast and glowering, with weighty clouds in shades of grey and only the very briefest of breaks. Houses give way to bungalows that crouch and hide from the wind. Ireland seems to me a land of bungalows, especially in the wilder parts. Many are new, with plastic windows, practical but downright ugly, and soon after Clonmany, with only a couple of miles to the beach, there are mobile homes that are uglier still.

I park up at the furthest end of the beach because there is a view of Súil Rock Binnion, which I read means 'the eye of the rock', though I don't feel I am being watched. There are few foolhardy enough to be here at this time of year, the day before Christmas Eve, with a brisk wind coming off the North Atlantic, though I can see figures in the far distance walking the sands. I have to say, it is beautiful, and desolate too. Perhaps I chose right after all.

Though, as I unzip the wheelie bag and take out the green plastic jar, the wind pulling at the door, I wonder if I am completely crazy. Thank the gods the Irish family don't know what I am up to.

It is already four o'clock, and if I am waiting for one of those shafts of sunlight to suddenly appear from the heavens, I might be waiting till spring. This all seemed straightforward in my mind, but now I am here, it has the banality of the real, and there is no epiphany, even when I try to force the feeling.

I pick my way over rocks and seaweed and keep walking until I have sand beneath my feet, clutching the jar with the ashes under one arm, then the other. It has weight to it. When I think I have gone far enough, I set it down on the beach and take a look around. No one. Or no one near enough to make any difference. There may be a couple of people over towards Binnion Rock, but they can't see much from that distance. Still, I'm embarrassed and not quite sure how to do this. And to think I could have been sunning myself in Varadero, the Caribbean flat calm in front of me, palm trees behind, and a bar on the beach serving cocktails of rum and coconut milk.

Because my father was a singer of songs, it crosses my mind to begin humming or singing out loud. There is no one to hear. I am alone, or alone with him. We never had a deathbed reconciliation; he was too far gone, and we didn't have the language for it anyway. But here and now, I could say a few words. I could say goodbye, and I could make the effort to remember him properly. That thought stops me in my tracks. What do I remember of the man?

The anger and the anxiety, yes, but that was not the whole of him, and the difficult later years have obscured his better self from me for so long. He had dreams and aspirations, many of which he fulfilled by escaping his upbringing in a loveless household and creating a family and a home of his own. And if his dreams were dashed and he became bitter and disappointed, I wonder now if much of that disappointment was with himself. Perhaps that was why he wanted to push me forward, to mould me in his image and see me succeed where he had failed, like so many fathers.

The man I see in the old photographs, kneeling beside his five-year-old son, who is blonde-haired and dressed like Rupert Bear, was not angry but proud. The man who spent his Saturdays after a long week at work refereeing football matches for the team he set up for me and my friends in the green strip of Ireland was the good father I have forgotten until now. The man with his arm around Mum, the two of them only in their early thirties, casually close, intimate, easy with each other, as only lovers are, was not anxious but happy and content.

All at once, I see us in the back garden of the old house, kicking a ball around together. The wooden pergola in front of the French windows was the goal. He was the shooter and I was goalie, and if I let one in, from time to time, a pane of glass would shatter and I'd hear my mother call from the kitchen to find out what was going on.

'Nothing!' he'd shout back. 'We're fine.'

'I heard glass breaking,' Mum would say, leaning out of the kitchen window.

'Shh!' he'd say to me, giggling and looking for all the world like a schoolboy himself. Then he'd whisper, 'We'll fix it later, the two of us.'

And we would. We'd go together to the shop and pick up a new pane, and I can see the tin of putty and the way he'd smooth it with his thumb and a kitchen knife, and show me how, and tell me about the skills I'd need to be a man, and how life was tough and I needed to be tough too. And when it happened again, because he kicked the ball too hard or I missed the catch, we'd cut cardboard to cover the missing glass until we could go back to the same shop and buy another pane. That man was not anxious or angry. He was my dad.

I don't know if he can hear me as I stand on the beach with the ashes before me on the sand, mute and inert. But I hope he can, because I have something to say.

'Do you remember the windows, Dad? I hope you

do, because I do. It wasn't all bad, not all of it, and it wasn't all your fault. Sometimes I make it sound like it was, but there was other stuff, wasn't there? I know your dad was pretty tricky, or so your brothers told me. You never wanted to talk about that. Maybe with good reason. We can't spend our lives blaming our mums and dads for everything, can we?

'So this is what I wanted to say … I let you down, I know that. I didn't pick up your mantle as you wanted me to. I didn't go for the business course in America, I didn't want to work for the man. I didn't buy a big house, climb the corporate ladder or join a golf club. And to be honest, I haven't done much else worthy of note. Sorry about that. But you let me down too, though mostly by being so hard on yourself. Sure, you were hard on me, but we didn't really get each other, did we? If only you could have accepted my help, leaned on me a bit, things would have been better. But it is what it is, and that's all ancient history now. That's why I'm here, that's why I've come to this place. To make peace. Because in our own way, we loved each other, you know? Neither of us was very good at showing it, but that's down to both of us. Anyway, it's done. Time now to forgive and be forgiven. Can we do that?'

I wait. My face is wet, though I'm sure it's the spray, and the only answer is the waves rolling in.

I don't know what else to do or say, so I pick up the

jar and head towards the waterline. The ripples of salt water are running under my shoes, and all at once they wash over and soak my socks. Wellingtons would have been sensible. But I just don't care, so I go a little further and give the jar a shake. I unscrew the lid and stand back like I've lit a firework as I wait for the swirling wind to reach inside and lift the ashes into the air in a magical plume of smoke. Only nothing is happening. The wind isn't doing what it should. I give the jar another shake and tip it towards the ocean, and all at once the ash is pouring out, sucked into the air, not a plume, but a fog of particles, snowing and swirling around my head and landing on my clothes. I don't want to breathe it in, so I take quick steps backwards, holding the jar at arm's length in front of me, until I stumble and fall, landing on my arse with a splash, feeling the sand sink beneath my weight and the icy sea seeping through to my skin.

Only then, with the empty jar in my lap, do I start laughing.

'What did you do?' asks my younger daughter, though she can barely speak for laughing. The empty plates from the Christmas feast have yet to be cleared, the glasses of wine are half full and there is more being poured. Phil is choking with laughter and holding his hand to his mouth to keep from spitting food. My ex is looking to the ceiling and shaking her head in disbelief. My elder daughter is reaching to hug me and the girls' boyfriends – Dan and Aaron – are no doubt wondering if I have altogether lost my mind.

'What could I do, except make my way back to the car, legs apart to stop the chafing of my jeans on delicate areas? Though you'll be glad to know I took the jar with me and popped it into the recycling bin at the pub. Then I cleaned myself up and went down to the bar. Which reminds me. I want to play you something. It's only recorded on my phone, but give me a second.'

'What about Nan?' asks my elder daughter. 'Isn't she still in the cupboard?'

'She's coming with me wherever I go next.'

'We're all coming with you, Dad; at least I am,' says the younger.

'Me too,' says her sister, and the boyfriends nod in agreement, as they have to when their love is tested.

I rootle about until I find what I'm looking for, and while I'm doing that, my sister wheels my mother back to the table after her nap. My ex is up clearing the dishes, so I call to her and she comes back into the conservatory, where we've set the table for the day, the same table I left tied up like a hostage in the garage all those months ago.

I press play. The lament of the fiddle hushes the crowd drinking at the Railway Tavern, and the young woman begins to sing of the grass that grows green around Ballyjamesduff, but I see another woman with a black shawl held tight against the wind, alone on the strand calling to her man lost at sea, and the voice I hear is that of a man singing of his loss and mine.

'Dad?' my elder daughter says.

'Ah, it's that song,' I say. 'Sure, I'm fine. Come on, let's raise a glass. To those we love, and those who love us. Absent friends and present company, and to the queen of ceremonies, Mum.'

I see Mum is saying something, but I can't hear the words. I ask my sister.

'She says get on with it.'

Phil and I are standing in the garden, sharing a smoke. I am supposed to have given up, and I have, only I'm making an exception today. I take a drag, and then another because I have missed it so.

I may have given the impression that Phil and I are similar creatures, when nothing could be further from the truth. He has a brain the size of a small island, and his theoretical understanding of anything from electrical systems in cars to wine production, music theory to philosophy is immense. We don't spend a lot of time comparing notes in these areas, because there's nothing I can do to compete. But I can make him laugh and there are things we have in common. A certain insouciance that has done us no favours in finding worldly success; a love of Frank Sinatra; and a fondness for chocolate. The two of us have spent many a happy hour putting the world to rights. Today, it's enough to be here together.

'What time will you leave?' I ask him.

'Early, I'm expected for lunch.'

'And you fly back to France when?'

'New Year's Day.'

'How is your mum?'

'Not bad. My sisters are there, and she's got someone coming in each day.'

We're quiet again, until I ask, 'What do you want for your old age?'

'Hadn't thought about it. Quick and dirty, maybe.'

Phil has only very recently broken up with a woman, ending a tempestuous relationship, but leaving him single like me, again.

'The way our love lives are going, it might be you and me seeing out our days together.'

'That's a terrifying thought.'

'I'm a carer now. Think about it.'

'I have. No.'

'How long have we known each other?'

'Too long.'

He hands me the smoke again. Just one more, then I'm done. For good.

'You old charmer,' I say, coughing and handing it back.

'Forty years. Forty-two, to be precise.'

'Is that all? Feels like a lifetime.'

Through the glass walls of the conservatory, Mum is surrounded by the family. My sister is feeding her spoonfuls of cut-up roast potato and tiny morsels of turkey, offering her a sip of wine from time to time. She is in the middle of life, just as I wanted her to be. That's something. Dan has his arm around my elder daughter, and Aaron is recording the younger on his phone as she sings her latest number. We can hear her through the glass.

'She sings like an angel, doesn't she?' I say to Phil, who knows about such things.

'She does.'

My ex is preparing plates for the pudding course to come. It is getting dark now, and the light from inside is all the brighter. What with the wine and the smoke, I might be imagining things, but there seems to be a special light to the scene. The light of a painting, with the woman in the wheelchair at the heart of it all, our very own chiaroscuro madonna.

I must be very drunk.

XXVI

It is January 13th, more than a year since I came back from France, eleven months since Dad died, and almost ten months since Mum came home. January is a dark month and I often struggle with the lack of light. Mum is already fast asleep, and I'm preparing vegetables to fry with the chicken.

There is some sad news. Uncle Pete has passed away, only a few months after moving to Devon to be with his family and his ex-wife. My younger daughter looked after Mum for a day and I drove down for the funeral. It was a hell of a journey there and back through sheets of rain, and I expected the worst. But the whole thing was oddly uplifting. It was good to see everyone, all of us transformed by age but still kicking.

My aunt phoned me a couple of days later. We had a giggle over the floods that had made the hearse half an hour late to the church. We both agreed that it felt like

Pete was still with us. She said the last three years, when they had seen a lot of each other and fallen in love again after decades apart, had been the happiest of their lives.

I choose to believe he is out there still, measuring twice and cutting once, cup of tea in hand. He is a man I loved. I haven't told Mum. I will when it feels right, but I talk about him whenever I can, just like I have done with Dad. The chat is always easy. Mum doesn't trip herself up on the boundary between the past and the present, between life and death, the way the rest of us do.

Today is significant because it is my sister's birthday. She is out tonight with friends in Vancouver. I spoke to her last night and she has news of her own. She got her long-awaited buyout from work. She is thrilled and scared. It is the end of an era, the end of a hard-working life, but also the start of something new. She is packing up the apartment already, and just needs a month or two to get her affairs in order before she comes back to live here and share the care. It's a big move for her, but she says it is what she's always wanted, to come home. I have to say, I am enormously relieved for myself and for Mum. I didn't want to let on before, but I was not sure how much longer I could do this alone.

By coincidence, today also happens to be Ellie's birthday. She is here now, having seen a clairvoyant this afternoon. I've bought a chocolate log – left on the shelves from Christmas, but I don't think she'll mind that – a smart T-shirt as a gift, and even got a card. We've moved from tea and cake to wine, and it's dark outside now.

'So tell me, what does the future hold?' I ask.

'She said she can see a man with a boat, so I've been wondering myself. I googled a boat show that's on in Southampton, and I'm thinking maybe I should go. I don't want to miss out.'

'Maybe take a stand and print some leaflets? You're good at marketing.'

'Funny.'

'So, from pilots to sea captains. Men with machines. Well, you're consistent, and he'll be away a lot too, so that will suit you. And tonight? What plans have you got? Is it the pub and too much Prosecco?'

'I don't think so, no.'

'So what *is* the plan?'

She says nothing, but she looks coy. I can't read her at all tonight. Maybe there is no plan.

'If you're at a loose end, you could stay and eat. But it's fajitas again, I'm afraid. Didn't we have them last time?'

'Always happy to be cooked for. Actually, I brought an overnight bag.'

I've got John Martyn playing, and I'm chopping red and green peppers as we chat. John is singing about rowing back down his river. It is a song I love and sometimes play very badly on my guitar. I'm thinking about the lyrics, so it takes me a moment to register what she just said.

'An overnight bag? I don't see it.'

'I left it in the car.'

I'm wondering why anyone would bring an overnight bag and then leave it in the car. So I stop chopping and turn around. I lean against the sink and study her.

'What?' she says.

'An overnight bag to see a clairvoyant and stop by with a mate for a cup of tea?'

She takes a sip of her wine; more than a sip. I might know where this is going, but I can't be sure. So I ask the question. 'Have I got this horribly wrong?'

'I don't know what you mean.'

'I think you do. Why do I get the feeling that I am somehow a part of your birthday present? Wasn't the T-shirt enough?'

She takes another sip and I reach for the bottle to pour more. She is meeting my eyes in a way she never has before.

'Well?' I ask.

'I haven't made my mind up yet.'

ACKNOWLEDGEMENTS

Writing a memoir means labouring alone to hammer experience into words on the page, but many skilled hands working together are required to make a book.

Jen Christie, my literary agent, was the first to see the potential of this story and to become my advocate, honing the idea, persistent and always supportive, even when my own courage failed. Thank you, Jen.

My editor and publisher, Claudia Connal, has been my guide and mentor through the writing process, her extraordinary patience and deft eye for detail transforming a rough manuscript into a burnished book. Thank you so very much, Claudia.

I am also immensely grateful to Yasia Williams whose bold design for the book's cover captures the intention and the ambition behind the words beautifully; to Emily

Brickell, whose input was always constructive and illuminating, and to Alex Stetter, Karen Baker, Hazel O'Brien, and the whole team at Octopus, who even as I write this are mustering their combined talents to steer the work to completion.

Alongside the professionals, I want to recognize family and friends who have so generously loaned me their lives that I might tell this story, especially Melanie, Ann, Pete, Jojo and Jenny. Without your tolerance, and especially your trust, there would be no book. To those of you who have retained your own names and those of you with new names, I thank you all from the bottom of my heart.

Phil, my oldest and best friend, has been stalwart at the end of a phone throughout, keeping my feet on the ground and taking my mind off things by sharing more than I will ever need to know about plumbing. Thanks, Phil. And a special thank you to Jax, who graciously allowed me to poach her persona for this story. Thanks, Jax.

Every wise writer – especially a new one – needs a good first reader, someone with a clear eye and sound advice. If that someone happens to love you for who you are, if not for every word you write, and happens to be a talented writer herself, you can count yourself fortunate indeed. And I do. Thanks, Carlotta.

I want to credit all our carers, those of you who have kindly permitted me to include you in the story, and those who have been there for us since; Lisa A, Claire, Trish, Sally, Linda, Lisa E, Debs L, Donna, Debbie J, Sharon, Sue, Helen, Pauline, Vicky, Maki, Caroline, Lisa K, Jenni, Zlatica, Zuzana, Joyce, Jackie, Hayley, Mel, Carmel, Jade, Clarissa, Debby P, Toni and Louise. If I have missed anyone, please forgive me, and know that I thank you all.

I would never have had the courage to set out on this enterprise were it not for the love of my family – my mum, my sister and my daughters in particular. I could not have made this dream come true without you. Thank you.